LIFE
LESSONS

How Jesus Guides Our Path
To Happiness In His Sermon
on the Mount.

GREG BURDINE

COPYRIGHT

Life Lessons: Lessons for a Happier Life – Jesus and the Sermon on the Mount

ISBN-13: 978-1548125127

ISBN-10: 1548125121

DEDICATION

This book is lovingly dedicated to my Lord and Savior, Jesus Christ. His greatest sermon has become my first book. It will take me my entire lifetime to apply its principles. But He continues to help me.

ACKNOWLEDGMENTS

First and foremost, I want to thank Jesus Christ for all He has done for me. Since receiving Him as my personal Savior as a young person, He has blessed me with wonderful opportunities and rewarding relationships. Yet, the best is yet to come.

I would like to thank my family, especially my wife Judy, for making my life such a joy. I am blessed way more than I deserve. My four children have brought me laughter, pride, and grandchildren. Thanks Jennifer, Joshua, Jill and Justin.

I am so thankful for my those who have been my pastor and have modeled servant leadership and Biblical preaching: Joe Lewis and his son, Marty Lewis, David Cavin, Bill Taylor, and Bill Dinoff.

I must express my appreciation to the people I pastor at Faith Baptist Church in Adrian, Michigan. I am still amazed that people want to hear me preach and follow my leadership. Yet, these people do. God bless them.

I also want to thank those who have helped me publish Life Lessons. My editor, Douglas Williams, has walked me through this process and been an absolute joy to work with. Several friends have been part of my Launch Team and I want to thank them for their help: Tim and Vicki Schmucker, Rick and Traci Arquette, Michael Burdine, Elias Correa, Kevin Davis, Ben Pearson, Rhonda Seneker, Jon Turner, Karen Wilks, Kirsten Yates, and Beth Zysk.

My passion is to help people follow Jesus better by learning the wisdom in the Bible. I hope this book has had a part in living a life full of blessing and happiness in your spiritual journey.

CONTENTS

PREFACE

A BANK PRESIDENT ONE day was going to retire. So, the company threw him a retirement party. The new bank president attended. In a conversation, the new president wanted to learn how to make good decisions. So, he asked the retiring president, "In my new capacity as president of the bank, I need to make good decisions. You seem to make a lot of good decisions. What's your secret?" The retiring president thought long and hard and finally said one word, "Experience." "That's a great and wise answer," the new president replied. "But how do you get experience?" Again, the retiring bank president thought long and hard. But this time he had two words, "Wrong decisions." It seems many learn how to live right by first living wrong.

What if you could learn how to live life right without making all the mistakes first? Wouldn't that be great? Just think of all the pitfalls and disasters you could avoid if you just did life right the first time. I suppose many of us wouldn't listen to such advice. But I think that deep down, all of us want to live the right kind of life. We just don't know how.

I've met a lot of people in my life. But I have never met anyone who wanted to fail in life. Deep down, most people want to have a great life. They want to have good families, have a good income, have good friends, have a good job, and have good health. Nobody wants to fail.

Most people want to live right. They want to love their family, be kind to their neighbor, give an honest day's work for an honest day's pay, and be the kind of person to others that they would have them be to them.

However, even though many people want to live right, most fail. For some, it's that they just don't know what they are supposed to do. I'm sure many people have not been brought up to understand the difference between right and wrong. Others may have experienced such a dysfunctional way of living that they really don't know how to treat other people. Yet, for many it's not that they don't know. They just don't know how. They have never seen right living modeled. The family structure greatly molded our former society. While this remains the primary influence in young lives, I think much of our society is more influenced by media. Yet, what is comical on television is often disastrous in real life.

We may want to have a good life. But selfishness, anger, pride and dishonesty often lead to a life nobody wants to have. Broken marriages, dysfunctional families, loneliness, and bitterness often result. This isn't the way we wanted our life to be. And this isn't the life we were meant to live. We were meant for more.

Whether they realize it or not, most people want to live out the Sermon on the Mount. Even if they are not aware, the principles of the Sermon on the Mount are ingrained in us all. I think God has placed in our society, if not in our DNA, the innate desire to live like God wants us to live. We were created in God's image and though we have sin, we still retain the likeness of God. The creation reflects our Creator.

There is a secret to living right. There is a key to be all God wants you to be and all you want to be. It is a key that will help you in your family, your job, your school, your church, your future, and with your friends and neighbors. The secret is to follow the instructions in the Sermon on the Mount.

When I bought my first car, I discovered in the glove box an instruction manual. I'll be honest, I never read it. I just wanted to drive my car. My priority was to make sure it had gas so I could go out and hang out with my friends. But I soon discovered that I needed to use my car like it was designed.

My vehicle instruction manual told me things like what kind of oil to put in the car, what replacement bulbs I should have, how to save stations on my radio, and even how to change my tire (and where the jack was). These came in handy when I needed an oil change, my tail light went out, my new girlfriend had a favorite radio station, and when I got my first flat tire. I once had a car that had the jack under the hood. I would have never found it without the instruction manual.

We would do well to follow God's instruction book, the Bible, as our guide to life. While the Bible is a big book with some complicated areas, the Sermon on the Mount is a concise three-chapter summary of God's way to live life.

My hope is that this book will help you know and live God's best for your life. If you can put just a couple of the principles from the Sermon on the Mount into your life, you will experience a more blessed life. Blessings on your journey.

INTRODUCTION:

READY TO PREACH

As I BEGIN this book on the Sermon on the Mount, a short introduction should help prepare you to discover God's plan for living right. My hope and prayer for this book is that you not only will discover how you are to live the life you've always wanted, but how to live the life God wants you to live.

The Preparation to the Sermon (Matthew 4:23-25)

"And Jesus went about all Galilee, teaching in their synagogues, and preaching the gospel of the kingdom, and healing all manner of sickness and all manner of disease among the people. And his fame went throughout all Syria: and they brought unto him all sick people that were taken with divers diseases and torments, and those which were possessed with devils, and those which were lunatick, and those that had the palsy; and he healed them. And there

followed him great multitudes of people from Galilee, and from Decapolis, and from Jerusalem, and from Judaea, and from beyond Jordan." (Matthew 4:23-25)

Jesus had three primary areas of ministry — preaching, teaching and healing. He performed these three functions from the beginning through to the end of His life. He began His ministry by presenting the message of the Kingdom and showing Himself to be the fulfillment of the Old Testament -promised Messiah by healing people (Isaiah 61:1,2). Matthew's Gospel can be partially outlined with an emphasis on three areas of Jesus' ministry: (1) Teaching (Matthew 5-7), (2) Preaching (Matthew 10-11), and Healing (Matthew 8-9).

Jesus had a public ministry. His public baptism by John launched His public ministry. He would continue to guard His private ministry with His disciples and His Heavenly Father. But He was called to minister to people. People responded quickly. Crowds began to follow Him everywhere. What Jesus said and did caused such a commotion that many wanted more. The crowds came from all over. Many came from nearby. But some came from far away.

At this early time in His ministry, Jesus chose to honestly present His claims. Thus, the Sermon on the Mount is similar to the "State of the Union" address of a new President of the United States. But this is more than what He hopes will happen to His people. This is what He expects from those who follow Him.

At the conclusion of the sermon, the crowds were aston-
ished at His doctrine and teaching. But the disciples not
only heard what He said, they responded to their Lord by
doing (Matthew 7:21). This sermon is not just a doctrinal
statement. This sermon is more than what ought to be in
the life of a believer. This sermon is not yet complete until
we do what it teaches.

The Purpose of the Sermon

Why did Jesus preach this sermon? As a preacher, it is important for me to understand the purpose of every sermon.
What do I want it to accomplish? What do I want people to
understand or do? A short summary of this great sermon
reveals two reasons Jesus preached it:

1. To show the inadequacy of man's righteousness (Matthew 5:20)

We all think we are right. Even if we admit we are wrong,
we do not think we are too wrong. We are slow to admit
our sins and weaknesses. So, Jesus sets up a comparison
of our sins in Matthew 5. He compares murder with anger,
adultery with lust, swearing with honesty, retaliation with
forgiveness, and love of neighbors with love of enemies.
While we may minimize our sin, Jesus concludes that we
are often more sinful than we acknowledge.

Jesus not only compares our sins, He also compares our
good deeds. I meet very few people who will not admit
they are not perfect. Our deeds, thoughts, and words reveal
a sinful heart. But in Matthew 6 , Jesus points out that of-

9

ten our good deeds are not really that good. Giving, praying, and fasting are all good things to do. But these good behaviors can be performed in a wrong manner. Rather than motivated by humility, these can be motivated by our pride. Instead of private performance, we can give, pray, and fast so others will notice us. In Jesus' day, as well as in contemporary Christianity, people often do good deeds so others will see them. This converts a good deed into a sinful deed. Even our righteousness is tainted with sinfulness and selfishness.

Jesus concludes His sermon in Matthew 7 by comparing the two forms of righteousness. There are two paths, two gates, two prophets, two vines, two trees, two confessions, and two houses. In each comparison, one leads to destruction while the other leads to eternal life. Jesus calls His listeners to reflect and recognize which righteousness they possess. Do you possess man's righteousness or God's righteousness? Often, man's righteousness looks like God's righteousness. But Jesus gives us clear vision into the hypocrisy of some good deeds. We need to turn from our own form of goodness and receive Him. It is only those who hear and obey His teaching who truly find the good life.

2. To proclaim the righteousness God expects

Throughout this sermon, Jesus makes comparisons and statements. He wants us to recognize that our righteousness is not good enough. God expects inward righteousness and this is impossible without God.

The Pharisees were trying to live a life by obeying all the commandments. They thought to go to Heaven they had to keep the commandments outwardly. But Jesus said a strong "NO." To go to Heaven you must keep His commandments inwardly as well.

It is not enough to not murder. You need to get rid of unjust anger. It is not enough to not commit adultery. You need to get rid of lust. To go to Heaven, according to Jesus, you need to be free of anger, lust, always practice honesty, forgiveness, and love your enemies. These are all inward attitudes that manifest in outward actions. We often flip the order and concentrate on the outward actions and assume the inward attitudes are the motivation. Not always.

It is impossible to change on the inside without the help of God. That is what conversion is. Conversion is an inward change that results in an outward change.

Jesus expects perfect righteousness. He tells us we are to be "perfect even as your heavenly Father is perfect." Wow! We are to be free of sin and full of righteousness. We are not to do anything wrong and we are to do everything right. Is that what He wants? Yes. Anything else is sin.

That is why the life God expects is impossible outside of Jesus. Jesus lived the perfect life. He did not lower the standards of perfection just so people He loved could make it. Heaven is a perfect place and only perfect people can go there. So, if we have sin or have not performed any good we should have, we can't go. Our righteousness is not adequate. But if we believe and receive Jesus Christ as our Lord and Savior, God will exchange our unrighteousness with Jesus Christ's righteousness. It is not that we ever get good enough. It is that we are given Jesus' righteousness.

The Problem of the Sermon: Can it be obeyed?

The Sermon on the Mount is undoubtedly one of the most famous and greatest sermon ever preached. We are fortunate that Matthew has recorded it in the most widely published book in history, the Bible. We are also fortunate that it is part of the inspired Word of God so that we are assured that it is not only an accurate account, but it is exactly what God would have us know.

But as many have sought to understand its meaning, there have been two opposite interpretations as to its application. These two applications determine our practical use of the Sermon on the Mount.

Many believe the Sermon on the Mount is to be kept exactly as it is given. So, in order to follow the teachings, they avoid oaths, personal or military force, and prohibit owning property. They withdraw from all political and social life and let the government take care of itself. They see the Sermon on the Mount as a list of behaviors to avoid and to practice.

However, it doesn't take long to see that it is nearly impossible to completely observe the Sermon's teaching. While we may be able to abstain from adultery and murder, it is very hard for anyone to keep from thoughts of lust and anger. And who can claim to be as perfect as our Heavenly Father? Surely no one would be so bold. So, I think it is too far a reach to claim that the Sermon was preached so that we would follow its teaching to gain Heaven.

So, since it is impossible to abide by the rules given, many teach that the practical application of the Sermon is for the millennial kingdom when Jesus literally reigns. This interpretation encourages a future obedience of all the commands and principles when the Christian's sinful nature will be completely removed and Jesus rules the world completely. They believe that this is just a preview of the world to come. So, they teach the Sermon is not for today, and only gives us a picture of God's ideal world.

But Jesus' model prayer tells us to pray "thy kingdom come, they will be done on earth as it is in Heaven." So, evidentially the kingdom of God is not yet in its fullness on Earth. So, I have a problem with limiting the application of the Sermon on the Mount to the future, millennial fulfillment. Let me share three ideas why the Sermon on the Mount is for today.

First, Jesus does not indicate or imply teaching for another age. He uses present tense verbs for His teachings. Jesus demanded that the people listening to Him at the time live the life He was commanding.

Second, Many of the teachings of Jesus in the Sermon seem meaningless in a future millennium. For instance, Jesus refers to peaceful and loving reaction to persecution and persecutors. There will not be persecution during the millennium.

Third, many other New Testament passages encourage a lifestyle of perfection similar to the teachings of the Sermon on the Mount. For example:

"But put ye on the Lord Jesus Christ, and make not provision for the flesh, to fulfil the lusts thereof." (Romans 13:14);

"Having therefore these promises, dearly beloved, let us cleanse ourselves from all filthiness of the flesh and spirit, perfecting holiness in the fear of God." (2 Corinthians 7:1);

"And this I pray, that your love may abound yet more and more in knowledge and in all judgment; That ye may approve things that are excellent; that ye may be sincere and without offence till the day of Christ." (Philippians 1:9-10);

"If ye then be risen with Christ, seek those things which are above, where Christ sitteth on the right hand of God. Set your affection on things above, not on things on the earth." (Colossians 3:1-2);

"Follow peace with all men, and holiness, without which no man shall see the Lord:" (Hebrews 12:14);

"But as he which hath called you is holy, so be ye holy in all manner of conversation; Because it is written, Be ye holy; for I am holy." (1 Peter 1:15-16)

I have a solution. This sermon gives us God's demands (not advice) on right living and we are expected to live to the letter of the law to enter His Kingdom (Matthew 5:17,18). But since we cannot live this life perfectly (1 John 1:8), we must come to God and receive forgiveness and new life through His Son Jesus (John 1:12). This regeneration (born again) makes us a child of God, as well as a citizen of the kingdom.

We are given a new nature. We have the enablement through God's ever-abiding Spirit to live up to the demands of the "Kingdom Standard of Living." Because we live in a sin-cursed world and still maintain a sin-cursed body, we will miserably fail in our attempt to live up to the kingdom standards. However, the divine nature now within us will continue to strive to help us live this godly life. If anyone is not living in accordance with the Sermon on the Mount, this reveals a life that is empty of Jesus, regardless of what a person may claim (Matthew 7:22-23).

Can the Sermon on the Mount be obeyed? Yes, through Christ. The key to living the Sermon on the Mount is to realize you can't live it yourself. Only Jesus Christ can live it through you.

"I am crucified with Christ: nevertheless I live; yet not I, but Christ liveth in me: and the life which I now live in the flesh

I live by the faith of the Son of God, who loved me, and gave himself for me." (Galatians 2:20)

As we begin this study through the Sermon on the Mount, it is important for you to settle how you will respond to its teaching. So even before we talk about the Sermon itself, how will you approach the contents? Are you willing to change whatever you think or behave in order to follow more closely to how Jesus wants you to live? Are you willing to give up any personal belief or behavior if God's Spirit presents you with a better pattern of life?

Will you pray the same prayer as young Samuel, "Speak Lord, your servant is listening?"

If you have not surrendered your life to God and trusted Christ for His righteousness, do it today. One day we will all stand before God in judgment. When our life is over, we must give an answer to the life we have lived. God gives life and He will demand an explanation on how we used it. So, have you lived the perfect life? I know I haven't. But I have trusted Jesus Christ as my Lord and Savior. I will never stand before God and receive His approval on my own behavior. I have disobeyed His law. I will only stand before Him based on my acceptance of His Son, Jesus Christ. You will never live your life well enough to inherit heaven. You must have perfect righteousness — Jesus' righteousness. Surrender your life to Him today.

If you have trusted Jesus Christ as your Lord and Savior and He is living in you, have you yielded your life to Him?

Allow Jesus to live His life through you. He died in your place. Now He wants to live His life through you. You may have yielded once or twice before. But living the Christian life is like driving a car that is out of alignment. Without constant attention, a car will begin to drift off the road. If you find yourself today drifting off the road you should be traveling down, turn back to Jesus.

If you have trusted Christ as Savior but you are definitely not living like a follower of Jesus, I encourage you to take an honest look at your life. Many people base their eternity on a decision they made years ago. We do not have eternal life because we made a decision. We have eternal life because Jesus saved our soul. I never want to encourage people to doubt their salvation. But I do think it healthy to test your salvation.

One day after wiring up a ceiling fan, I had to test it to see if it was wired correctly. Even though I thought I did everything right and it looked good, I needed to turn the power back on and check it out. If it worked, I did it right. If nothing happened, or worse, I knew the wiring was wrong. Fortunately, the fan worked and my home project was complete.

If you are not living a life pleasing to God, it could be like faulty wiring. Maybe you thought you did all the right things, but life isn't working for you. Maybe you have never truly repented of your sins and trusted His Son for salvation. At the very least, if you are disobedient, you are in danger of severe discipline from your Heavenly Father. At the worst, you have convinced yourself that your eternity is secure when it is actually in jeopardy. Double-check your salvation.

CHAPTER ONE:

BE HUMBLE

P OVERTY IS ALL around us. In the big cities, we can see the face of poverty at intersections with signs of 'Help Needed.' Even in my small town, we have small tent villages of the homeless behind our local K-Mart.

A stigma is attached to the poor. Sophie Tucker once said, "Listen. I've been rich, and I've been poor. And believe me, rich is better." But Jesus pronounces His first blessing on the "poor in spirit.' This is the first beatitude and is the foundational attitude we must have. No one enters God's kingdom without having the attitude described here.

"Blessed are the poor in spirit: for theirs is the kingdom of heaven." (Matthew 5:3)

What does it mean to be 'Poor in Spirit'?

Jesus does not pronounce a blessing simply on being poor. But He does proclaim that the "poor in Spirit" are blessed. To understand what this means, it may help to understand what it does not mean.

"Poor in spirit" does not mean poor in material possessions. Jesus did not say "Blessed in spirit are the poor." Poverty is not a blessing in itself. The Bible does tell us that often riches make it harder to follow Christ. Wealth has kept many people away from the Gospel. However, many godly people in the Bible were wealthy, including Abraham (Genesis 13:2), David (1 Chronicles 29:28), Solomon (2 Chronicles 9:22), Hezekiah (2 Chronicles 32:26-28), and Joseph of Arimathea (Matthew 27:57).

"Poor in spirit" does not mean poor-spirited. Special blessings are not given to those who lack enthusiasm. Solomon encourages *"whatsoever thy hand findeth to do, do it with all thy might" (Ecclesiastes 9:10).*

"Poor in spirit" does not mean someone who is a coward or lacks courage. Several times throughout Scripture we are commanded to have *"good courage"* (Deuteronomy 31:6; Joshua 1:7-9; Psalm 31:24).

"Poor in spirit" does not mean to have a low view of oneself. Though Scripture commands us not to think too highly of our self (Romans 12:3), nowhere does it command us to think poorly of our self. As humans, we are all created in the image of God and bear a likeness to Him, even in our sinfulness. Oftentimes, in order to appear to be humble, people put themselves down. But this is not what it means to be "poor in spirit."

"Poor in spirit" does not include sacrificing our individuality or personality. We are each a unique person, with specific characteristics that make us our self. In no way should a person become what they are not in order to be blessed. Surely, we should change sinful behavior and we may want to curb certain personality quirks. But we are not to be molded into the same "cookie cutter" type of person as someone else. A look at the variety of early disciples that Jesus chose should encourage diversity of personalities within the family of God.

So, what is 'poor in spirit?'

"Poor in spirit" is the opposite of being rich in pride. To be rich means to have more than you need. Too many of us have way more pride and selfishness than is sufficient.

"Poor in spirit" is not just normal poor — it is begging poor. The Greek word used is ptokas, not the typical word for poverty (penance). Ptokas is to be so poor you have to beg. It is to have a spirit that has absolutely nothing to offer and must beg God to be filled. We can't bargain with God in our spiritual life. We are completely bankrupt, with no deposits of our own. The only asset we have is a poverty-ridden spirit.

"Poor in spirit" is an emptying, while the rest of the sermon is a filling. This first line of Jesus' sermon sets the stage for everything else. Unless we admit our spiritual poverty, we can never receive anything else God has to offer. All the other blessings are dependent on the attitude of complete humility.

"Poor in spirit" condemns the idea that we can live the sermon ourselves. Someone has said, "This Sermon on the Mount is too high to climb. Any attempt or idea that you can live the sermon is proof you do not understand it." It is only when we admit our defeat and utter helplessness and hopelessness that God will begin to cultivate in our life the character depicted in the rest of the sermon.

"Poor in spirit" is completely opposite of most people's thinking. Pop culture thinks we must build up our self-image. I've heard many counselors say that the reason we have so many emotional problems in our world is because of low self-image or low self-esteem. But that is where we need to begin. Without God, we have nothing, we can do nothing worthwhile, and we are nothing. We are spiritually empty. Our spirits are so poor we must beg in order to live. We often hear of being "filled with the Spirit" (and this is important). But few talk about being "empty of the spirit."

"Poor in spirit" is admitting your need. If you think you have no needs, that is your biggest need. The first step of Alcoholics Anonymous is: "We admitted we were powerless over alcohol — that our lives had become unmanageable." To be "poor in spirit" is to admit that we have nothing in which to make ourselves acceptable to God spiritually. It is to beg Him for spiritual help.

How can the begging, humble be blessed?

The "poor in spirit" are blessed because they have a disposition that is the very opposite of human nature. It is a sure sign of a divine work of grace. Blessings follow those who are in a position to be blessed. Those who are humble will be exalted and blessed (Matthew 23:12).

The "poor in spirit" are Christ-like and anything Christ-like brings blessing. Jesus always did what His Heavenly Father desired. Even when He was hungry, He refused to turn stones into bread. It is not that Jesus thought less of Himself. It is simply that Jesus did not think of Himself. He knew who He was — the Son of God. But He refused to use His position to gain some kind prominence over others. He even washed the disciples' feet as an example of His humility.

The "poor in spirit" will one day be kings. Today, we are servants of the Kingdom. Tomorrow the servants will rule as kings with authority. Those who are "poor in spirit" right now (present tense) possess the kingdom. But they behave as servants of the kingdom. One day the humble will be exalted.

How can you tell if you are humble?

"Humility is that grace that, when you know you have it, you have lost it."– Andrew Murray

Four ways you can tell if you are "poor in spirit" …

1. You accept others, because you have accepted yourself.

2. You accept your circumstances.

3. You have a right attitude toward things.

4. "A man is rich in proportion to the number of things which he can afford to let alone." – Thoreau

5. You accept God's will for your life.

Pride is a terrible attitude. The Lord resists the proud, but gives grace to the humble. Even though the world may not tolerate nor applaud the humble, the Lord does. Humility is the first step into the Kingdom of Heaven.

Have you ever humbled yourself before the Lord God Almighty?

Is your life a life of humility before others?

CHAPTER TWO:

BE SAD

EVERYONE LIKES TO laugh. It's contagious. Jerry Lewis once said, "The people of the world who have the ability to laugh at themselves are those who survive." The Bible says, *"A merry heart doeth good like medicine" (Proverbs 17:22).*

The world's philosophy is: "Smile, smile, smile!" But Jesus says, "Mourn, mourn, mourn."

"Blessed are they that mourn: for they shall be comforted." (Matthew 5:4)

What is Jesus telling us in this second beatitude? What kind of mourning is He talking about?

Jesus and Sorrow

God cares about your sorrow. He really does. This second beatitude proves it. He notices when you hurt. Jesus gives a special blessing on those who mourn and cry. I believe when we hurt, He hurts. What hurts us hurts Him. He really cares about what we care about.

Your sorrow is okay (Ecclesiastes 3:1-2, 4). Some people think it is a sign of weakness to cry. But God created us to cry. God even cries at times. Mourning is an expression of our love for others. Often at a funeral I spend time with families who are overcome with grief and sorrow. It is almost as if they can barely breathe. But I've expressed to them that we cry because we love. And the deeper we love, the deeper we cry. To remove the tears, we would need to remove the love. So, it's good to cry. It shows we love. God has promised that He will comfort those who mourn. Comfort cannot be received until we have really mourned.

Sorrow is an important aspect of life. We find many people in the Bible cried. Abraham cried when his wife died (Gen. 23:2). David cried over his loneliness (Ps. 42:2-3). Timothy cried in discouragement (2 Tim. 1:3-4). Jeremiah cried as he preached (Jer. 9:1). Paul cried as he taught (Acts 20:31). A father cried over his son (Mark 9:23-24). A woman cried tears of devotion at Jesus' feet (Luke 7:37-38). I once had to break the news to two young boys that their father had been killed in an automobile accident. One reacted by crying uncontrollably. The other tried to hold it in and not show any emotion, just a few tears. Over the course of many months, the boy who cried was able to adjust to the loss. However, the boy who held it in had troubles. I think it was because He refused to mourn over the loss of his dad. Sometimes you just need a good cry.

Most mourning will not go on forever. In this beatitude, Jesus promises a time of future comfort. At the moment of intense loss, it seems like we'll never be the same. I remember when my dad died. It seemed like I cried all the time. But as time went on, my mourning turned to fond memories. Even today, I have times of intense pain because my dad is no longer with me. But God has given me great comfort. Time does heal our emotional wounds.

Jesus offers blessing to those who mourn. For those who follow Jesus, something good will come from our tears, so it's okay to walk through sorrow. This is not a natural response. Normally people do not want to confront anything that may cause them sorrow. People deliberately turn from anything unpleasant, especially if it makes them sad. Sometimes we make having "fun" such a high priority that we don't do anything that causes sadness. If it doesn't make me laugh, we think it's boring. But Jesus gives a blessing to those who mourn.

What kind of mourning is Jesus talking about?

Natural sorrow can bring comfort. Human sorrow teaches us to appreciate good things. It increases our sensitivity to others, especially their needs. It teaches us to be better people. Sorrow and grief reinforces the fact that this life is not all there is. And sometimes it drives a person to God. Natural sorrow is good. But I don't think Jesus is primarily talking about natural sorrow.

The Greek word Jesus used here for "mourn" is the strongest of the nine words used for grief. It is the morning over someone who has died — a deep, inner agony you can't hide. It is definitely associated with the first beatitude. Humility and sorrow go together. Just as the first beatitude speaks of spiritual poverty, this beatitude speaks of spiritual mourning. It is sorrow over sin. Jesus tells us there is a blessing to those who mourn over sin, for they shall be comforted.

Jesus is talking about sorrow over sin. It is an emotional reaction to the first beatitude. When a person sees his spiritual poverty, he can react in one of four ways:

1. He can deny it.

2. He can admit it and try to change.

3. He can admit it and give up.

4. He can admit it and turn to God.

Many people know they are sinners, yet never mourn over that fact (Zech. 12:10). But the attitude of mourning over sin is called repentance. It is a change of heart over our sinful condition. Instead of being happy with sin or trying to hide sin, it is a sorrow and confession of sin.

How will mourning over sin bring comfort?

A person who truly mourns over their sin will confess it to God. This brings God's forgiveness. There is great comfort in knowing that Jesus forgives all sin.

A person who truly mourns over their sin will be given power to overcome those sins. God's Spirit will help you battle the temptations that entice you into wrong. You can live a life of less sorrow if you turn from sin to God. Sin brings sorrow, but forgiveness of sin brings blessing.

A person who truly mourns over their sin will eventually live in Heaven. In Heaven, there will be no sin. In Heaven, every tear will be wiped away. In Heaven, we have eternal comfort!

Do you experience sorrow over your sin or do you just try to hide it? Only those who admit their sins and seek Jesus will find inner peace and comfort.

CHAPTER THREE:

BE GENTLE

WE HAVE FOUR children. I can remember when we brought our youngest (and last) child home from the hospital. The children were all older and Justin was a little baby (though he was near 10 pounds). They wanted to play with their younger brother, but we cautioned them, "Be gentle." They needed to treat this little newborn with gentleness. This is the idea behind the word "meek" in Jesus' third beatitude.

"Blessed are the meek; for they shall inherit the earth." (Matthew 5:5)

Doesn't this beatitude sound ridiculous? It is opposite of today's society. We think that it is the high-energy, powerful, pushy person who inherits the earth. A few years ago, I saw a best-selling business book called, Leadership Secrets of Attila the Hun. Many modern-day leadership ideas follow the same model. But this beatitude goes against all popular theories of success. Jesus tells us that, to be successful, we must be meek and gentle.

Does this beatitude mean we are never to speak up and defend ourselves? Does this mean we should allow ourselves to become doormats and let people trample over us? I don't think this is what Jesus meant by meek.

It may help you understand what meekness is by learning what the Greek word means. The Greek word Jesus uses for meekness is praus. Aristotle used this word to describe the balance of two extremes. For example, in the area of money, some people spend way too much. The opposite extreme is a miser, like Scrooge. The balance would be a generous person. To Aristotle, the balance between too much anger and no anger at all was praus.

During Jesus' time, praus was used to describe good medicine. Too much medicine would kill you and too little wouldn't do anything. It was also used to describe a gentle breeze. Too little and it wouldn't move a ship; too much and it would sink one. It was used to describe a colt that had been broken and domesticated. The young horse was potentially dangerous, but tame. It was used to describe a power that was under control. This is what our English word meekness means — power under control.

Our society has the wrong perception of meekness. Meekness is not idleness or laziness. Nor is it simply being a nice person. To be meek is not weakness in personality or character. And it is definitely not being a pushover or doormat for people to walk over. Meekness is controlled power.

What is meekness?

Meekness is a balanced attitude about oneself. It is a true view of oneself, expressing itself in right attitudes toward others. Alternatives to meekness include mild, gentle, patient, long-suffering, ready to listen and learn. I have often discovered that if a person has a correct view of themselves, it will give them a correct view of others. But if you think you've been cheated in life or are better than others, this will often reflect negatively against others.

Meekness is a natural following of the first two beatitudes. When a person really sees them self as spiritually impoverished (1st beatitude) and mourns over that sin (2nd beatitude), there is a personal recognition that nobody can say anything about him that is too bad. He is amazed that God and others can think of him and trust him as well as they do. Meekness starts with you.

Meekness is being honest with yourself. But being honest with yourself about sin is not the same as letting others be honest about your sin. We may be a sinner, but we do not want anybody else to say we are a sinner. However, being meek is a realization that without Christ we have no righteousness or goodness of our own. As a friend of mine always says when someone asks him how he's doing, "Better than I deserve."

Why is meekness so important?

Meekness is a virtue. It is a personality trait we all should strive to live. Jesus was meek (Matthew 11:29). To be meek is to be like Jesus. Meekness is a fruit of the Spirit (Galatians 5:22,23). It is evidence that the Holy Spirit is in control. Meekness should characterize our response to God's truth (James 1:21). It is the spirit we are to have when we witness to others and share the Gospel (1 Peter 3:15). It is the spirit we are to have when we deal with problems among other people (Galatians 6:1).

"Anyone can become angry, that is easy. But to be angry with the right person, to the right degree, at the right time, for the right purpose, in the right way – this is not easy."
– Aristotle

The meek will inherit the earth.

The world associates happiness with worldly possessions. People believe that the way to gain worldly possessions is through ability, strength, hard work, self-assurance and at times assertion. But Jesus says the meek will inherit the earth. Notice, the meek will not win the earth, but they will inherit the earth. It will be given to the meek.

There is a spiritual aspect of the inheritance that meekness rewards (Psalm 37:11, 16). The meek man is the man who is truly satisfied and therefore content (James 1:3,4). When you are meek, you want nothing for yourself. When you want nothing for yourself, God gives you everything. Meekness is the secret of possessing everything.

There is also a literal inheritance that the meek will receive (1 Corinthians 3:21-22). Psalm 37:1-11 tells us that the meek are actually promised the earth. Romans 8:16-17 says we will inherit the earth with Christ. One day the meek will rule the world.

CHAPTER FOUR:

BE HUNGRY

H AVE YOU EVER been real hungry or thirsty? I have. It's not a pleasant feeling and we try to eat or drink something to rid ourselves of that feeling. But Jesus promises a blessing to those who are hungry and thirsty for righteousness.

"Blessed are they which do hunger and thirst after righteousness: for they shall be filled." (Matthew 5:6)

People cannot be satisfied with things, ideas, or even other people. We were created for more. Our deepest needs and desires can be met only by a fellowship with God Himself. People hunger and thirst after God. But they try to fill it with things and people.

"Thou has made us for Thyself , O Lord, and our heart are restless until it finds its rest in Thee." – Augustine of Hippo, Confessions

This is the true test of your Christian experience. Do you hunger after God? Is the deepest desire of your life to have a right relationship with God? If so, you are truly blessed because you will be filled. I want to look at the key words in this passage and find out how to find fulfillment in life.

What are we to be?

We are to be hungry and thirsty.

Spiritual hunger is a real hunger. It is as real as physical hunger but different. Just like physical hunger, it keeps on until it is satisfied. It does not pass away. It may get more intense. We may not feel it as much during certain times. And many people try to ignore the hunger in their heart. But it is still there.

It is an intense hunger. The way the Greek word is used in this verse means hungering for "all" the righteousness. It's like saying, "I'm so hungry I could eat a cow." It is a starving hunger. In Jesus' parable of the prodigal son (Luke 15:11-32), He mentioned that when the prodigal son was hungry, he went to feed on the husks. But when he was starving, he turned to his father. God often uses this deep spiritual hunger to pull us to Himself.

What are we to be hungry for?

We are to be hungry for righteousness.

We sometimes hunger for the wrong things. Lucifer hungered for power (Isaiah 14:13-15). Nebuchadnezzar hungered for praise (Daniel 4:29-30). The rich fool hungered for pleasure (Luke 12:16-21).

But it is important to be hungry for God and His righteousness. The definition of righteousness is "to be right with God." Righteousness means to be holy. It is to be like Jesus. It is to be free from the penalty, desire, and presence of sin. Even though we all fall short of holiness, I think everyone has the hunger for it deep within him or her.

But some people don't appear to hunger for righteousness. It seems they hunger for sin. Why do some people not feel spiritual hunger? Even some Christians do not seem to be hungry for righteousness.

I think we don't hunger for righteousness for the same reasons our bodies don't hunger for food. Hunger is normal. But some things disrupt our natural hunger.

Sometimes you aren't hungry because you are sick. When you aren't feeling well, you lose your appetite. And when you're getting better, you regain your appetite. Sometimes we aren't spiritually hungry for righteousness because we are spiritually sick. It may be we are not truly a Christian. It also may be due to being unhealthy in our Christian life. A healthy Christian is a Christian that hungers for God's righteousness.

Sometimes we aren't hungry because we don't exercise. I have discovered that if I work hard or exercise, my appetite increases. Because I have used more energy, I need to replace my energy. I remember when I was younger and exercised all the time, I could eat a full meal and be hungry in just a couple of hours. If you find you're not as spiritually hungry as you should be, maybe you need to exercise more. A good spiritual exercise is to share the gospel with others. Nothing will create a hunger to draw closer to God and discover His righteousness than interacting with those who need to receive the gospel.

Sometimes we aren't hungry because we have spoiled our appetite. I've done this way too many times. When I get hungry in between meals, I will sometimes eat a candy bar. This stops my hunger, but it's not a real healthy hunger control. There have been a few times I've stopped at McDonald's on my way home for dinner, and stopped just to get a small order of fries or hamburger. It's not surprising that I'm not hungry for dinner. That can get you in trouble at home. It can also get you in trouble spiritually. When you spend your hunger feeding on the wrong things, it often has disastrous results. When you have that restless, deep down hunger for God, you need to go to God, or the Bible, or at least God's people. But when you sense a spiritual hunger, and try to appease it with television, entertainment, or anything else but God, you will lose spiritual strength. This often leads people to drift away from God and the church.

Sometimes we aren't hungry because we are too busy. Have you ever spent time doing something and simply forgot to eat. You were so absorbed in what you were doing that eating was the last thing on your mind. It's easy to do. Hours on the computer, or working out in the garden, or any other activity that grabs your attention will make you forget you're hungry.

Sometimes that happens spiritually. We can get caught up in something and not even notice that we should be feeding our soul. What occupies our time isn't always necessarily bad. Sometimes it's good things that keep us from God. Sports, family, work, and even ministry can keep a person from gaining spiritual nourishment from God and His Word. I often equate spirituality with activity. As long as I'm serving hard for God, I must be living for God. But the easiest place to drift away from God is the church pew (or even behind the pulpit). Don't let your work for God keep you from your relationship with God.

How are the hungry happy?

The hungry are happy because they are filled.

Hunger isn't a happy experience. But hungering for righteousness will eventually bring happiness. How? Happiness is a result of living right. God blesses the righteous. So, when we hunger for righteousness, God will fill us and we will be blessed.

Happiness, like pain, is a by-product of something else. For example, when you have a disease, you may experience pain. Getting rid of the pain does not get rid of the disease.

To permanently remove pain, you must remove the disease. Even so, people try to get happiness. But it is a by-product of righteousness living. You will never find lasting happiness by looking for it. It will be just out of reach. Happiness only comes when you are hungering and thirsting for righteousness.

Many try to find happiness in drugs, sex, education, family, or travel, or any number of other methods. But they will never find lasting happiness in things. They will only find partial satisfaction there. The writer of Hebrews reminds us that there are *"pleasures of sin for a season"* (Hebrews 11:25). The only true happiness that does not pass away is in Jesus Christ.

Many Christians are searching for the ultimate Christian experience. They travel from church to church, concert to concert, seminar to seminar; listen to speakers; or read books to find what they think other Christians have. If you want a happy experience, you will never find it by looking for it. It only comes by hungering and thirsting after righteousness.

I have discovered an interesting difference between physical and spiritual hunger. Physically, you are either hungry or full. But spiritually, you evidently can be both. You can have a hunger that really can't be completely filled until you get to Heaven. I think that is what Jesus does to me. He fills me but I want more.

Everyone has emptiness, a desire, and a hunger that needs fulfillment. A person can search their whole life to find peace, contentment, prosperity, and happiness and never find it. Like a starving man, they will try it all — good and bad. But Jesus gives us the only answer — "Happy are those who are starving after a right relationship with God — for only they will be happy and satisfied." The answer to all your desires and longings is being right with God.

Do you hunger after Christ? Do you want Him more than anything else in the whole world? I hope so. This is the only way to be satisfied and find contentment in your life.

CHAPTER FIVE:

BE MERCIFUL

THIS IS JESUS' fifth beatitude. The first four beatitudes deal entirely with inner principles… principles of the heart and mind. We've discovered the blessing of humility, meekness, gentleness, and desire for righteousness. These are concerned with the way we see ourselves in relation to God. The last four are outward manifestations of those attitudes. We will discover the blessing of mercy, holiness, peacemaking, and persecution.

Each of the first four beatitudes parallels the last four beatitudes. Notice this:

- Those who are poor in poverty of spirit recognize their need of mercy and are led to show mercy to others.

- Those who mourn over their sins are led to purity of heart.

- Those who are meek always seek to make peace.

- Those who hunger and thirst for righteousness are never unwilling to pay the price of being persecuted for righteousness' sake.

I want to show you the blessing of mercy. Mercy is desperately needed as a gift from God for the salvation of every person. In addition, just as God is merciful to us, He requires us to follow His example by extending mercy to others.

"Blessed are the merciful: for they shall obtain mercy." *(Matthew 5:7)*

What is mercy?

Negatively, some see mercy as a weakness. One person has called mercy a "disease of the soul." Some people make decisions (sometimes wrong decisions) to prove how tough and unmerciful they really are. The idea is that if you don't look out for yourself, no one else will. So never give in to anybody else.

Positively, mercy is a godly attribute. God is merciful. God's mercy is the attribute that appears when we deserve His punishment, but He doesn't punish us. Rather, He blesses us. In mercy, God suspends condemnation. In the Bible, God extended mercy to Solomon (1 Kings 11:13) and to the nation of Israel in captivity (Psalm 106:45). In the Old Testament, God's mercy was best illustrated on the Day of Atonement, when the high priest would enter the Holy of

Holies in the Temple to offer a sacrifice for the nation of Israel (Leviticus 16:14).

God's mercy can be better understood by contrasting three similar attributes: love, grace, and forgiveness. God's love is constant, but His mercy is given in time of need. God's grace gives (positive), but God's mercy helps (negative). God's forgiveness forgives sin, but His mercy is for any and all trouble. Mercy is the attitude that helps the afflicted and rescues the helpless.

How to show mercy?

We can show mercy to others in many ways. I will just name three.

First, we can show mercy in physical actions. The Good Samaritan is a shining example of someone who showed mercy by physical actions (Luke 10:25-37). After being passed by two religious men, a man who had been beaten and robbed was approached by a man of Samaria. This Samaritan bound up his wounds, put him on his own animal for a ride to a place to stay, and paid any expenses to bring him to good health. Much like the Good Samaritan, we can help people in their distress and difficulties by offering practical help. Giving money, home projects, fixing a car, visiting in the hospital, sending an encouraging card, are just some of the ways we can extend mercy.

Second, we can show mercy in our attitudes. This is where mercy begins, the heart. When you see someone in a difficulty, your first attitude should be compassion. We want to help. A merciful attitude will find some way to alleviate their discomfort. But even if we cannot ease the pain, we can genuinely express our heart's desire. True mercy does not hold a grudge against someone or find some kind of enjoyment when they go through a tragedy. Even if there is a past hurt, mercy has no resentment. Though one may fall or be caught in a sin, mercy does not publicize the wrong-doing, but offers help.

Third, we can show the most mercy through spiritual activity. In particular, we can be a soul winner. The worst that has happened to any person is sin. Sin is the most destructive aspect of anyone's life. *"The wages of sin is death" (Romans 6:23)* and will lead to eternal damnation. We can show mercy to the unsaved through pity, confrontation, prayer, and proclamation of the Gospel. The most merciful action you can do for another is share with them the good news of the Gospel that forgiveness of sin is available through the blood of Jesus Christ.

Primary Result of Being Merciful – Receive Mercy

Jesus promises mercy for those who extend mercy to others. Does this mean we earn mercy (forgiveness) by being merciful? If we forgive others, will God forgive us? The simple answer is "No." I know we have many verses that seem to argue against this. *"With the merciful thou wilt shew thyself merciful..." (2 Samuel 22:26).*

Let me see if I can explain how this works. Mercy begins with God. In a degree, everyone receives mercy from God. We live because of God's mercy. We are saved because of God's mercy. Now that we have received His mercy, we are expected to extend mercy to others. Being merciful to others is a logical reaction and loving recognition that we have received mercy as a gift from God. Mercy is not a natural attribute of humanity. But it is a response to a gift of mercy. Especially those who have received the gift of salvation are able to extend mercy to others. We do not earn salvation by being merciful. But mercy is a result of the salvation we receive.

The cycle of God's mercy is as follows: (1) God is merciful to us by saving us through Christ. (2) We are merciful to others because God has been merciful to us. (3) God gives us more mercy, pouring out blessings and withholding chastening. (4) We continue to give mercy to others in practical ways because God has continued to be merciful to us.

The Bible says, *"He that hath pity upon the poor lendeth unto the Lord; and that which he hath given will he pay again" (Prov. 19:17)*. A beautiful illustration of mercy is that of Joseph and his brothers. Through jealousy, the brothers sold Joseph into slavery and convinced their father that wild beasts had killed him. In the following years, through his faithfulness to God and his masters, Joseph rose in position in Egypt from slave until he was second in power to Pharaoh himself. A famine drove his brothers to Egypt to buy food. Joseph recognized them, dealt with them with wisdom and compassion. Finally, his father and all the family traveled to Egypt where he could feed them through the remaining years of famine. Joseph had every right to be angry with his brothers. But Joseph showed mercy and love. Why did Joseph do this? Because those who are shown mercy will show mercy and will be happy.

If you want to be happy, it will not be because you are angry and judgmental. Happiness and blessing are given to those who have experienced the mercy of God and show mercy to others.

CHAPTER SIX:

BE HOLY

W E LIVE IN a wicked world. Often, we are ashamed of what we read in our newspapers and hear on television. Immorality and violence are all over our society and in our media. Part of the tragedy is that much of America seems to enjoy it. Our most popular reality shows are simply a parade of people at their worst. We are in great need of purity in our world today.

But if there is any institution in our society that ought to represent God's purity, it should be the church. Yet, scandals seem to be just as prevalent among God's people as in the secular world. It was Peter who proclaimed, *"For the time is come that judgment must begin at the house of God..." (1 Peter 4:17).* This was in the first century. I'm sure it is much worse in many congregations. Even in church and among believers we need purity.

Jesus pronounced a special blessing on those whose hearts are pure.

"Blessed are the pure in heart: for they shall see God."
(Matthew 5:8)

"Pure in Heart"

I want us to look at these two words. This will help us understand what Jesus means by "pure in heart."

What does Jesus mean by 'pure'?

Pure means clean. The word was also used to describe un-mixed milk, gold, wheat (Jeremiah 32:39). If something was pure, it was not diluted. It was genuine. Today, we might consider a "pure heart" as a person with integrity or character. This describes a person who is the same whether you meet them in church or on the job. They are the same whether it's Sunday or Saturday. They are not two-faced. Only you and God know if you really are who you appear to be. And sometimes you can fool yourself.

What does Jesus mean by 'heart'?

The Greek word is kardia, where we get our English word "cardiac." It refers to the inner person. People are tri-une, like God. God is a unity of three persons: Father, Son and Holy Spirit. You are a unity of three entities: spirit, soul, and body. The spirit is that part of you that relates to God. In the unbeliever, the spirit is dead and must be made alive by the Holy Spirit. The soul is your mind, will and emotions. It is the part of you that thinks and feels. The body is the physical organs and systems that make up your physical appearance. It is your five senses. Your heart is your soul, the center of our emotions and thinking. It is the real you.

"Pure in heart" encourages us to be "pure" in our motivation. What is your motivation for what you do? What's behind it? Is it for money? Selfish desires? It is not only important to have "pure" actions, but our motives should be "pure."

"Pure in heart" encourages us to be "pure" in our integrity and character. Character is what you are when no one is looking. It is not something you show others, but it is how you behave behind their back. Reputation is important, but we should be more concerned with our character than our reputation. Our character is what we really are, while our reputation is merely what others think we are. Abraham Lincoln once said, "Character is like a tree and reputation is like a shadow. The shadow is what we think of it; the tree is the real thing."

"Pure in heart" encourages us to be "pure" in holiness. When Peter listed the steps toward spiritual maturity, the second step following faith is "virtue" (character) (2 Peter 1:5). When someone becomes a new Christian, we often try to get them to do things. Christian service is important, but more important than service is character. Holiness is extremely important in the Christian life. Without "holiness," no one will see the Lord (Hebrews 12:14).

The Result of a 'Pure Heart' is to 'See God'

The tragedy with much of Christianity today is Christians are satisfied with mediocre living. Many are simply satisfied with being better than the ungodly world. Few Christians really want to be holy. C.S. Lewis once said, "It is safe to tell the pure in heart that they shall see God, for only the pure in heart want to."

I'm afraid that too many of us do not want to be pure in heart. Just like the nation of Israel begged to go back to the "onions" of Egypt, many Christians cling to the sinful, selfish lifestyle of an unbeliever. But the "pure in heart" will be able to see God. The "pure in heart" will see God in others, see God in circumstances, and see God working in their own life. They will one day see God in Heaven.

But you can't be pure in heart by yourself. Our heart is naturally wicked. *"The heat is deceitful above all things and desperately wicked: who can know it?" (Jeremiah 17:9)*. Our problem is our heart convinces us that we are pure enough. But our heart deceives us. I am my own worst enemy. I am not a good judge of my own character and heart. Others can help, but primarily we need God. God will clean our heart. Solomon asks, *"Who can say, I have made my heart clean, I am pure from sin?" (Proverbs 20:9)*. As our heart is clean, God allows us to see Him. And as we see God, He will change us even more to be what we should be.

So how can we develop a clean heart?

We can develop a clean, pure heart by faith (Acts 15:9). We are made pure by faith and faith comes by hearing the Word of God (Romans 10:17). I encourage you to read the Bible. Just like running water cleanses the rocks in a stream, simply reading the Bible will do wonders to clean your heart. Read it, study it, memorize it, hear it preached and taught by gifted teachers, meditate on it throughout the day, and teach it to others. You can find many ways to allow God's Word to build your faith.

We can develop a clean, pure heart by the blood of Jesus (1 John 1:7,9). It is the blood of Jesus that cleanses and forgives our sin. When Jesus died on the cross, His shed blood was the payment of your sin debt. As you keep your sins confessed before God, it is a constant reminder that those sins are forgiven. Ask the Holy Spirit to reveal any unclean actions, thoughts or words. As He reveals these to you, confess and agree that these are sins.

When your heart is pure, you will see God. The Greek word for "see" means a continuous looking. The "pure in heart" will continually behold God. It is amazing that, as you live out your life, you will see God in creation. It's beautiful! Take a look outside and watch the sunrise or sunset, look at the stars, look in the mirror and see the wonderful creation in your own face. Isn't it amazing that you can see so many wonderful things with the eyes God created for you? What about your mouth? God created a tongue that tastes so many wonderful foods. And you can talk to so many people about anything? What about your nose? God made your nose so that you can smell a beautiful flower or the perfume your husband or wife is wearing. The pure in heart will see God in creation.

When your heart is pure, you will see God in your circumstances. Not every circumstance is godly. But God will give you vision to see His hand in everything that happens. I remember when I failed as a church planter in Columbus, Ohio. After less than three years, I had to leave because it just wasn't working out. I felt so bad. But in less than three years, I understood why God brought me through it. At Faith Baptist, we had a church fire and had to rent a school. It was exactly what I had been doing for three years in Columbus. God was in my failure.

When your heart is pure, you will see God in His Word. The Bible can be a difficult book to understand. After all, One who knows everything authored it. But I think God opens the best insights into His Word when our heart is pure.

When your heart is pure, you will finally see God when you arrive in Heaven. It is going to happen. If you are a Christian, you will see God. You will spend forever with Him and worship and praise Him forever. You will get to serve Him as He created you to serve. It will be wonderful. Practice now by being pure in heart.

How to stay clean

Once you have a clean heart, or at least are seeing your heart become more pure, there are a few things you can do to maintain your purity…

1. Pay close attention to what you look at. Often temptations come through our sight. Obviously, pornography is one way we can be tempted. But there are many other things that our eyes can look at. We see it and want it. The first temptation was through eyesight by a woman looking at beautiful fruit (Genesis 3). Be careful what you allow your eyes to see.

2. Give greater thought to the consequences of sin. You can't emphasize the consequences of sin enough. The worst-case scenario may just happen. We often think that our thoughts aren't as bad as our action. And in reality, they aren't. But thoughts turn into action if not guarded. Guard your thoughts.

3. Begin each day with a renewal of reverence for God. I always try to start my day making a list of five things for which I'm thankful. Then as I review the Lord's Prayer, I ask God to lead me not into temptation. I want a pure heart and I ask God to help me keep it pure. Prayer will keep your heart clean.

4. Periodically, in the day, focus on Christ. I try to have a private time with God in the morning because once my day begins, it's hard to get the quiet time back. But I often try to take a few pauses throughout the day to recheck my heart. With reminders available on your phone, it might be good to have a notification

set to bring you back to think about Jesus. Keeping your thoughts on Jesus will assist in keeping your heart pure.

Jesus demands that we do right in our heart. Check your motivation, your integrity, and your holiness. Whether anyone notices or knows about your holiness, Jesus sees it.

What if a U.S. Presidential candidate knew something about an opposing candidate that would guarantee, if the public knew, he/she would win, but it would jeopardize national security? Do you think he/she would have enough integrity to keep it a secret? I doubt it. With all the mudslinging in politics, it seems personal advancement is greater than personal integrity.

But one former candidate remained true to America. In 1944, Presidential candidate Tom Dewey understood that the government cracked the Japanese code in 1941. This meant that his opponent, President Franklin Roosevelt, must have known about the attack on Pearl Harbor. If Tom Dewey exposed this fact, Japan would know that the United States knew their code and much of our future ability to intercept and understand information would have been lost.

In Tulsa, Oklahoma, he wrestled with whether to tell the public what he knew. The Chief-of-Staff came to his motel room with a letter asking him, in the interest of the war, to keep silent. For the sake of national security, he decided not to share what he knew and eventually he lost the election to Roosevelt. He never told what he knew. In 1981 all this information was released to the public and for the first time American knew that the U.S. had cracked the Japanese code before the attack on Pearl Harbor. But the code cracked was the diplomatic code, not the military code. Nobody knew about the attack. FDR did not know. Japan's premier did not know. Japan's minister of war did not even know. Tom Dewey probably went to his grave wondering if he did the right thing. But now we know he did.

Do you have a pure heart? Or do you have a heart filled with anger, selfishness, or lust? I hope you will turn to Jesus to clean your heart and stay close to Him to keep it clean.

CHAPTER SEVEN:

BE A PEACEMAKER

MANKIND IS EVER searching for peace. In the last 4,000 years, it has been said that there have been less than 300 years of peace. A visitor from Mars would say that Earth's chief industry is war.

When Dr. Robert Oppenheimer, the designer of the atomic bomb, was asked if there was a defense against the bomb, he said, "Yes, Peace." Apollo 11 had a motto — "We come in peace for all mankind." They left it on the Sea of Tranquility. Ironically, Neil Armstrong and Buzz Aldrin found themselves in a peaceful place because there had never been any humans there before.

Albert Einstein once said, "The unleashed power of the atom has changed everything except our way of thinking. We shall require a substantially new manner of thinking if mankind is to survive." When asked, "So you don't believe there will ever be peace?" he responded, "As long as there will be man, there will be wars."

People have tried to find peace in society through treaties, negotiations, financial pressures, gun control, knowledge, and even religion. But there is no real peace in the world until there is peace with God. Man's conflict with man is but an expression on the human level of his conflict with God. The history of man is full of futile efforts to live happily and peacefully apart from God.

There is peace only in God

"But now in Christ Jesus ye who sometimes were far off are made nigh by the blood of Christ. For he is our peace, who hath made both one, and hath broken down the middle wall of partition between us." (Ephesians 2:19-20)

There are over 400 references to "peace" in the Bible. Six times in the New Testament God is called the "God of Peace." So, let's take a closer look at peace and being a peacemaker.

"Blessed are the peacemakers: for they shall be called the children of God." (Matthew 5:9)

1. We must first be at peace with God

"Therefore, since we have been declared righteous by faith, we have peace with God through our Lord Jesus Christ." (Romans 5:1).

There is a bumper sticker that says, "No God, No Peace. Know God, Know Peace." Isn't that true? Our first place to seek peace is with God. That is the reason Jesus came to earth. Because of sin we are at war with God. From the time sin entered our world in the Garden of Eden, humanity has been at odds with God. Our sin and His holiness are not compatible. They are not at peace but in conflict.

But through Jesus, peace has been made. Through Jesus we can be justified by grace through faith. When a person believes in Jesus and accepts His salvation and forgiveness, peace results with God. The barrier of sin has been removed. This eternal peace with God is a great gift available to all who trust Jesus as Savior.

Is everything okay between you and God? Have you trusted His Son, Jesus Christ, as your own personal Lord and Savior?

2. We then can have the peace of God

"And the peace of God, which surpasses every thought, will guard your hearts and minds in Christ Jesus." (Philippians 4:7)

Life can be anything but peaceful. But peace is an attitude that every Christian can experience. God knows the unrest we feel within ourselves. He knows the broken world around us and the anxiety that overcomes us. But He has promised that when we have Jesus, we have peace.

Paul tells us that the "peace of God" is beyond anything we can understand. The peace of God is stronger than our world and circumstances. God's peace fills us when everything is going wrong. God's peace is stronger than anything you must face. I've discovered three things you can do to have the peace of God.

First, to have the "peace of God," you must quit fighting God.

"Peace I leave with you, my peace I give unto you: not as the world giveth, give I unto you. Let not your heart be troubled, neither let it be afraid" (John 14:27).

God has given us His peace, but often we fight Him. I've met people who are so accustomed to turmoil that they don't know how to live in peace. If the day seems to be peaceful, they have to bring up some kind of drama to create an environment of chaos. Quit fighting God's peace.

Second, to have the "peace of God" you must surrender to God.

"Now be ye not stiff-necked, as your fathers were, but yield yourselves unto the Lord, and enter into his sanctuary, which he hath sanctified forever: and serve the Lord your God, that the fierceness of his wrath may turn away from you." (2 Chronicles 30:8).

The Jews were in a continual rebellion against God. But, like them, if you want to enter into peace, you must surrender to God. The sanctuary was a peaceful place in the Temple and God invited them to enter that place. In the passage above, I find it interesting that part of the chaos people were experiencing was due to the wrath of God. Some of our problems will be immediately eliminated if we will simply yield to God.

Third, to have the "peace of God" you must serve God. Not only does 2 Chronicles 30:8 teach us that we must surrender to God, but we must serve God if we want His peace. I can't tell you the inner tranquility that comes when I serve God. He has blessed each of us with talents, abilities, and experiences. They are given to us to glorify Him. But most people serve themselves. We use these gifts to make money or make ourselves happy. But when you use what God has given you to make Him known and serve Him by serving others, it will give you more peace and joy than you can imagine.

To have peace with God and the peace of God is not enough. We are to be peacemakers.

3. We must be peacemakers

Okay, so we can have peace with God and the peace of God within. But what about all the situations around us? What about the circumstances we can't change, the relationships that are broken, the chaos we can't calm, the hurts we can't heal, the violence we can't understand? What can we do about the need for peace in the world we live in?

This is what this beatitude calls us to do. We are called to be peacemakers. The very presence of a Christian in our world should make it a more peaceful environment. So, how can we be a peacemaker? Let me share with you two things you can do to be a peacemaker.

First, to be a peacemaker, you must control your own anger (Matthew 5:21-26; 18:15-17; Proverbs 18:19). How can you help others in conflict, if you cannot help your own conflict? When I was younger, I had a big problem with anger. It seemed like when I hit a certain level, I couldn't control my rage. I don't know how others deal with it, but I prayed a lot. I asked God to help me with my anger. And He did. I still can get very angry, but it takes a whole lot more to set me off. If you want to be the peacemaker in any situation, you must be able to control your own emotions.

Second, to be a peacemaker, you must have peace with your enemies (Matthew 5:38-48; Romans 12:18-21). We must not let our "enemies" control our thoughts, emotions, and decisions. It's easy to let others get under your skin and bother you. Sometimes just the thought of another person will bring up negative emotions. The best way to have peace with your enemies is to pray for them. I'll get to this later, but pray that God's will be done to them, that they do God's will, and that God would bless them. It will do you good. Bitterness doesn't hurt the other person. It hurts you. If there is someone who is your enemy, pray for them and do them good.

Why are we not effective at making peace between God and man?

I think too many Christians are not peacemakers. One reason for not being a peacemaker is that we choose not to get involved when we see disagreements. It's a lot easier and less messy to just stay out of it. After all, we weren't asked to intervene. But positive peacemakers are often proactive.

A second reason we are not peacemakers is that we have no common ground with our opponents. One of the reasons we get in disagreements is we don't see eye to eye. It's important to see a situation or relationship from the other person's viewpoint. Make every attempt to try to understand before being known.

A third reason we are not peacemakers is we are at fault. One of the most insightful verses in the Bible is everyone *"did that which was right in his own eyes" (Judges 17:6)*. The reason most of us do what we do is we think we're right. It takes a lot to convince us we're wrong. So, we often try to be peacemakers by changing the minds of everyone else. But, in reality, we are the ones who need to change. Ask yourself, "Could I be wrong?" When you admit you are wrong, it is amazing how fast peace will result.

Christians are called by God to be peacemakers. Is your work, your school, your community, your home a more peaceful place because you are there? Or do you add to the disruption and fighting? Does it matter if you are there or not? Do you effectively change your environment to a peaceful one? Do you find solutions to problems or do you add fuel to the fire? Do you bring people together on common ground, or do you separate people and their differences?

CHAPTER EIGHT:

BE A MARTYR

THE PERSECUTION OF Christians can be traced histori-
cally from the time of Christ through the present. In
many places in our world, it is dangerous to claim the name
of Christ. Even in America, Christianity has felt negative
pressure from society. But Jesus pronounces a blessing on
those who are persecuted. Maybe the idea of being a martyr goes a little too far . But if you aren't willing to die for
Christ, you will probably not be willing to be persecuted
for living for Him.

"Blessed are they which are persecuted for righteousness'
sake: for theirs is the kingdom of heaven. Blessed are ye,
when men shall revile you, and persecute you, and shall say
all manner of evil against you falsely, for my sake. Rejoice,
and be exceeding glad: for great is your reward in heaven:
for so persecuted they the prophets which were before you."
(Matthew 5:10-12)

This is the 8th and final Beatitude. It is as if Jesus said, "If you live like this, people will persecute you." Why are good people persecuted? Why do bad things happen to good people? Paul reminds us, *"Yea, and all that will live godly in Christ Jesus shall suffer persecution." (2 Timothy 3:12)*

Reasons for Persecution

Before I present some reasons why Christians are persecuted, I need to be honest. Some of the problems Christians face are not always persecution. Sometimes it is God's judgment for wrongdoing. Sometimes it is not due to the "offense of the cross" but due to the "offensive" behavior of the Christian. And sometimes Christians face "persecution" because of poor judgment and foolish decisions. So, before you think you are being persecuted, make sure you humbly look within.

However, I discovered three good reasons a Christian may face persecution.

First, the Christian life runs opposite to the way of the world. It's like going the wrong way on a busy highway. You're going to get hurt. People don't like it when you don't act like everyone else. You might face persecution because you don't blend in.

Second, Jesus said we might be persecuted for "righteousness" sake. When you live right, some people don't like it. When people want to do the wrong thing, they don't want someone around to make them look or feel guilty.

Third, Jesus also said we may be persecuted for "His name's sake." He also said, *"But all these things will they do unto you for my name's sake, because they know not him that sent me." (John 15:21).* When we identify with Jesus, we may be treated like He was. Jesus lived the perfect life and was kind and compassionate to everyone. Yet, they took Him and crucified Him. Don't be surprised when you try to live like Jesus that they treat you like Him.

Response to Persecution

How should we respond when we feel persecuted by others? The most natural reaction is to treat people the way we've been treated. But as followers of Jesus, we are to respond correctly to persecution. Do not react, resent, or retaliate. Treat people like Jesus treated them.

"Forasmuch then as Christ hath suffered for us in the flesh, arm yourselves likewise with the same mind: for he that hath suffered in the flesh hath ceased from sin;" (1 Peter 4:1).

Three good responses should be part of our reaction to persecution:

1. **Reign** (Matthew 5:10). We need to act as kings, above the circumstances. People with low self-esteem react quickly and defend themselves. But people of royalty and etiquette treat others with respect.

2. **Rejoice** (Matthew 5:12; 1 Peter 4:14; Acts 5:41). Realize it is a privilege to be persecuted for Christ's

sake. It may give you new opportunities to witness for Christ (Acts 1:8). For sure it will give you an opportunity to grow (Psalm 119:67; Hebrews 12:2).

3. **Release** (Matthew 5:43-48; Romans 12:14, 17-21). Love, pray, act. Forgive others for their bad treatment of you. If you are not careful, the hurt will cause a bitterness that will hurt you way more than the original hurt. I've met Christians who have allowed a person to continue to hurt them long past the event. Don't let anyone have that kind of negative power over you. Pray for them. Do good to them. Release them from the control they have over your life.

Rewards for Persecution

God rewards us for our persecution. There is a double mention of "blessings" to this beatitude of persecution.

First, there is a reward now. There is a story in the Old Testament that is an encouragement to me when I'm feeling negative pressure from someone. David was running from Jerusalem because of the revolt of his son, Absalom. A descendant of Saul, Shimei, was cursing David. One of David's men, Abishai, requested to kill him. But David said something surprising. He said, *"Let him alone, and let him curse... It may be that the Lord will look on mine affliction, and that the Lord will requite me good for his cursing this day" (2 Samuel 16:12-1).* It seems that there is a special blessing that God gives when we are persecuted.

Second, there is a future reward (Matt. 5:12; Mark 10:28-30). In spite of persecution, Moses was blessed (Hebrews 11:26). In spite of persecution, Abraham was blessed (Hebrews 11:10). Throughout the Bible, blessings are given to those who are persecuted. *"If we suffer, we shall also reign with him..." (2 Timothy 2:12).* *"For I reckon that the sufferings of this present time are not worthy to be compared with the glory which shall be revealed in us" (Romans 8:18).* They may take away everything we possess in this world, but no one can touch anything God has given us in the next.

Ignatius once said, "Nearer the sword, then nearer to God. In company with wild beasts, in company with God."

W.C. Burns of India said, "Oh, to have a martyr's heart, if not a martyr's crown."

CHAPTER NINE:

BE A WITNESS

EVERY CHRISTIAN IS a witness and has an evangelistic lifestyle in a world that desperately needs Jesus. Jesus gave us two pictures that describe our lifestyle in relationship to a lost world.

"Ye are the salt of the earth: but if the salt have lost his savour, wherewith shall it be salted? it is thenceforth good for nothing, but to be cast out, and to be trodden under foot of men. Ye are the light of the world. A city that is set on a hill cannot be hid. Neither do men light a candle, and put it under a bushel, but on a candlestick; and it giveth light unto all that are in the house. Let your light so shine before men, that they may see your good works, and glorify your Father which is in heaven." (Matthew 5:13-16)

The Salt of the Earth

Jesus describes Christians as salt. There are many uses that describe both salt and the Christian.

1. **Seasoning** – Many foods taste better with salt. Eggs, potatoes, vegetables, meats are seasoned with salt to bring out the flavor. Christians flavor the world. Christians are to bring out the best in the world. The world is a better place because of the presence of Christians.

2. **Antiseptic** – Salt is a cleansing agent. I remember when I got my wisdom teeth removed. The doctor told me to wash my mouth out with warm salt water. It would help clean my mouth. Salt also helps filter and purify. We use salt to purify our water. Christians are meant to be a cleansing agent in our world. We should be cleaning up the sin and filth in our communities. When God was going to destroy Sodom and Gomorrah because of their continued sin, He agreed to halt the destruction if ten righteous people were found among its citizens. Sadly, fewer were found and the city was destroyed. This illustrates the point that godly people should be cleaning up the communities they live in.

3. **Irritant** – Salt as an irritant reminds me of the old saying, "It's like pouring salt in a wound." Sometimes I've had a cut on my finger and grabbed some potato chips. Ouch! The salty chips hurt my finger. Sometimes Christians will become an irritant to an ungodly community. It can be irritating to have

someone who wants to do right when you want to do wrong. But Christians are not called to be sugar to soothe, but salt to convict. This doesn't mean we irritate just to be irritating. There are too many people like that. But it is the message of Jesus and His cross that often will irritate people.

4. **Preservative**. I think this is the primary reason Jesus illustrates believers as salt. Before the days of refrigeration, it was difficult to keep meats without spoiling. One way to preserve meat was to wash it with salt. The salt would prevent spoiling. Salt works by drying the food to remove any way for water bacteria to grow. Christians are to preserve the world by holding back the decay of this world. Our world is getting worse and worse. But Christians are encouraged to combat the evil in the world and slow down the decay.

Salt does its work because of its chemical composition. Salt is made up of sodium chloride. You really can't see salt work, but you can see its effects. Like salt, the work of Christians is often hidden. Our personal character, prayer, and silent influence will do a work that often is unnoticeable. But salt changes whatever it touches. Salt, like character, is a hidden work.

Christians are the "salt of the earth" but sometimes we are ineffective.

*   **Saltless Salt.** Jesus talks about salt that has lost its saltiness. It is worthless but to be thrown out on the

street. It took me a while to figure this one out because pure sodium chloride does not change its composition. So how can salt lose its saltiness? In Jesus' day, people got rock from the salt mines. Sometimes the rock salt would contain impurities. If left out, the pure salt might leach out and all that was left was the rock. In this parallel, Christians are like rock salt. We have impurities and if we are not careful, we can we can lose our effectiveness sitting on the shelf. It is often gradual and impossible to reestablish. Saltless Christians are rejected by Christians and the world.

- **Saltshaker Christians**. To be effective, salt must come in contact with another substance. Salt does not work at a distance. Rebecca Pippert has written a great book called, Out of the Saltshaker and Into the World. This illustrates the problem that many Christians have. They never come in contact with the people who need the Gospel. But this presents another problem, contamination. One of the challenges of serving Christ is having contact with sinners without contamination. But we must connect with the unsaved to reach them for Christ.

The Light of the World

Jesus also illustrates the Christian life as a light. We are the "light of the world." Now, in John 8:12, Jesus called Himself "the light of the world." So now in His absence, Christians are the Light of the World. In reality, He is still the Light and we are a mere reflection of Him. The better people see Jesus in us, the better testimony we will give them.

As you think of light, you can't help but think of the great light, our Sun. And those of us who are Christians are like the moon. At night, the moon is the light in the absence of the sun (though the sun is never really absent, just unseen). So, like the moon, Christians are the reflection of the "real" light. I found several similarities between the moon and Christians.

1. The Moon is a dead planet. We were dead in our sins but made alive through Jesus Christ.

2. The Moon reflects the sun's rays. The moon has no light of its own. But it shines because of the sun.

3. The Moon bears the craters of the past. Even with the naked eye, one can see evidence where meteors damaged the moon. Christians still show evidence of sin's damage. But this gives us an opportunity to share about God's forgiveness.

4. An eclipse occurs when the world gets between the sun and the moon. It doesn't happen very often, but sometimes in the middle of the day, the sun will disappear behind the moon. If Christians get between the lost and Jesus, they won't see Him at all. We need to get out of the way. A lunar eclipse occurs every month. When the earth gets between the sun and the moon, the moon appears dark. When we allow the world to get between us and Jesus, soon His light may disappear. He is still there, but we have allowed the world to take His place.

5. The Moon is the same size as the sun, from the perspective of Earth. This is how we can have both an eclipse of the sun and of the moon. Though the moon is much closer, they are the same size from our perspective. To many of the unsaved, we are the only Jesus they will ever see. We know that Jesus is much better than we are, but we are much closer to them. Christians need to live a testimony and witness before our friends so they will see Jesus living through us.

Light, to be useful, must be seen. Jesus talks about the foolishness of keeping a light under a basket. It does little good. Light is to be set high so others can see it. The light we have (Jesus) is to shine so all can see.

I discovered a few principles about shining the light of Jesus. I hope these will help you let your light shine.

- People are confused in the dark. Everything looks distorted. That's why many people do the things they do. They live in the spiritual dark. One of the terms Christians use for those who are not Christians is "lost." Most don't know they are "lost," but they are. They are like someone wandering around in the dark. Someone needs to shine a light. It doesn't need to be a bright light. Just a little light will shine brightly in a dark room.

- Only we can hide our light. A light doesn't force itself. A light just shines. But you can hide the light. Like a child who tries to read a comic book under the covers away from the eyes of his parents, many Christians don't want their friends to know of their faith. But don't hide the light. Allow people to see and hear about Jesus in your life.

- Our light shines brightest at home. The closer you are to the light, the brighter it is. Our Christian faith should be seen best by those who know us best. This is often our family. Our family should be our best evidence to others that Christ is Lord of our life. That is why pastors and deacons are required to have faithful spouses and children. These are evidence of true faith. Shine the love of Jesus to your family.

One of my favorite books about evangelism is 'How to be a Contagious Christian' by Bill Hybels and Mark Mittelberg. Our church has used it as a strategy for church-wide outreach. In the book, the concept of Christians being both salt and light appears. Salt represents our character. Light represents our works. Both are needed to be an effective witness. God's evangelistic strategy in a nutshell is: God desires to build into you and me the beauty of His own character (salt), and then put us on display (light). Let your light shine!

CHAPTER TEN:

KNOW GOD'S WORD

I HAVE A BROTHER who is 15 months younger than me. We were pretty much the same size throughout our lifetime. I remember in a closet in our house in Franklin, Ohio, my mom made a measuring chart. We would stand next to it and she would measure how tall we were. I would often ask her to measure me to see if I was getting taller. I remember stretching my neck upward so I could be just a little bit taller.

As a follower of God, I want to "measure up" to God's standard. I definitely am not perfect. But I inwardly have this strong desire to do the right things and not do the wrong things. I hope as a follower of Jesus Christ, you have this same desire. Actually, I think one of the tests of whether you are truly a Christian is whether you have the inward desire to be more like Christ.

But, in reality, we will never in this lifetime "measure up" to God's standard. The reason is because His standard is perfection. As Paul reminds us, *"All have sinned and come short of the glory of God" (Romans 3:23)*. Every person who has ever lived has missed God's mark.

Throughout time, God has given to humanity some of the measurements He is looking toward. Basically, if God says "No," we shouldn't do it. And if God says, "Yes," we are commanded to do it. Even in the perfect environment, God had one rule. In the Garden of Eden, God told Adam not to eat of the fruit of the tree of the knowledge of good and evil. Yet, Adam and Eve both disobeyed and suffered the consequences.

To the Jewish nation, God gave many rules. The most famous are the Ten Commandments. When the New Testament refers to these rules, they are called "The Law." God gave these laws to help His people know how He wanted them to live and be blessed.

But nobody could keep these laws perfectly. Even today, many refer back to the Ten Commandments as one of the greatest summations of good living.

Many accused Jesus of breaking the Law. Though He did not do anything wrong, He often disregarded some of the Jewish customs. So, at this point in His sermon, Jesus wanted to make sure His followers and His critics knew His stance on the Law.

Jesus and the Law

"Think not that I am come to destroy the law, or the prophets: I am not come to destroy, but to fulfill." (Matthew 5:17)

This might be the most extraordinary statement in the whole "Sermon on the Mount." Jesus is laying down the eternal character of the Law. Again and again, Jesus broke what the Jews considered the law. He did not observe the hand washings that the Law laid down. He healed sick people on the Sabbath, although the Law prohibited such healings. He was, in fact, condemned and crucified as a law-breaker. Yet, here He seems to speak of the Law with a respect and reverence that no Pharisee or religious leader could match.

Jesus did not destroy the Law, He fulfilled it

Most of Jesus' listeners had a wrong perception about His teaching. They thought Jesus was anti-law. Both by His actions and His condemnation of the Pharisees' hypocritical keeping of the Law, many questioned His respect of the Law. But Jesus came into the world on a mission — to fulfill Scripture.

"Fulfill" means "to fill." The Law had created a hole. The Law revealed a vacuum in the lives of people that left emptiness. People cannot keep God's Law perfectly. We often cannot even keep our own laws.

But when Jesus came, He filled the hole that the Law revealed. Jesus filled the teaching about God, the prophecies, and the righteous demands of the Law. Christ fulfilled the

Moral Law by His holiness, the Civil Law by His death, and the Ceremonial Law by His sacrifice.

Jesus did not change the Law, but re-emphasized it

"For verily I say unto you, Till heaven and earth pass, one jot or one tittle shall in no wise pass from the law, till all be fulfilled." (Matthew 5:18)

Jesus believed in the permanence of the Law. The Law would not change. He was not just a believer in the thoughts and words of the Law. Jesus believed that the letters and even the smallest markings were permanent.

Jesus mentions a "jot" and a "tittle." These are small markings on Hebrew letters. A jot (jod) was a Hebrew letter that looks similar to our apostrophe. In many Bibles, you can see a jot in the title over Psalm 119:73. But even more amazing is the tittle. A tittle was just a little mark at the top of a Hebrew letter. In these same Bibles, you see a tittle by comparing the Hebrew letter "daleth" in the title over Psalm 119:25 with the Hebrew letter "resh" in the title over Psalm 119:153. The only difference in these two letters is a small, almost imperceptible mark on the top. That is a tittle.

Jesus prohibited even small changes of letters in the Law. I am not a fanatic about the danger of various translations of the Bible. But I do think it is important not to mess with God's Word. It's not just the thoughts or even the words that are important. Jesus emphasizes even the value of letters and marks. The Bible was important to Jesus. Throughout the rest of the chapter, He will comment on the depth of the meaning of the Law in our lives.

The Law & the Religious Leaders

The Old Testament consisted of broad principles. Some laws were permanent throughout societies, such as "Thou shalt not kill." Others were only within the Jewish community, such as the prohibition against eating certain meats. And some laws were ceremonial and helped with the sacrificial system God implemented to atone for sin.

The religious leaders (scribes) tried to make interpretive laws to apply these commands to every situation. Jesus called these further rules and regulations "traditions" because they were passed orally to each generation of scribes. In 300 A.D., they were written down to form the Mishna (800 pages). Later, Talmuds were written to explain the Mishna (The Jerusalem Talmud had 12 volumes. The Babylonian Talmud had 60 volumes). This resulted in thousands of laws good Jews were expected to keep.

For instance, the Old Testament Law prohibited work on the Sabbath. So, scribes tried to define work. How much can a person pick up? How far can a person walk? What occupation can a person do? These were written down as traditions and soon occupied an importance equal to the written law.

The Pharisees of Jesus' day tried to keep all these laws and would often add more laws. Often, the "traditions" seemed to be harder to keep than the Law. However, these traditions actually made the Law easier to keep because they reduced God's Law to external obedience. God's Law always requires inward as well as outward obedience. This led the religious leaders to focus on outward obedience and neglect inward obedience. As long as a person kept the outward law, they were okay. They would major on the minors, and minor on the majors. This was always a source of contention between Jesus and the religious leaders.

The Law & Salvation

Laws are good but no one is saved by keeping the Law (Gal. 3:24). The problem of keeping the Law for salvation is you need to keep all the Law. It is like a chain. If you have 10 links in a chain, but one of them is broken, the chain is broken. Unless someone can keep all God's Laws, they cannot be right with God.

The Law cannot make anyone right. The Law can only show that we are wrong. The Law is like a mirror. It can show us that our face is dirty. But it has absolutely no power to wash our face. The Law is good, holy, and righteous. But it has no power to make us good, holy, or righteous.

If God's Law (10 commandments) cannot make a person righteous, neither can any of man's traditions. The purpose of the Law was to show that, to please God and be worthy of citizenship in His kingdom, more righteousness is required than anyone can possibly have or accomplish by and in himself. We must receive the perfect righteousness of Jesus.

The Law and the Christian

"Whosoever therefore shall break one of these least commandments, and shall teach men so, he shall be called the least in the kingdom of heaven: but whosoever shall do and teach them, the same shall be called great in the kingdom of heaven. For I say unto you, That except your righteousness shall exceed the righteousness of the scribes and Pharisees, ye shall in no case enter into the kingdom of heaven." (Matthew 5:19-20)

Though keeping the Law cannot save us, it is important for us to keep and teach the Law. Negatively, we should not break the Law. Just because we cannot keep the Law perfectly doesn't mean we are free to break the Law. The Law was given not only to show that we are lawbreakers, but also to guide us to live a good life. We must not loosen ourselves from its requirements and standards.

Positively, we must obey and teach the Law. The Law is good. It will help us live a better life. But personal obedience is not enough. We must teach others to obey. This is discipleship.

As we seek to obey and teach God's laws, it is important to understand the difference between "least" and "great" commandments. Scripture makes clear that not all commandments are of equal value (Matt. 22:37-39), but none are to be disregarded.

We also must know the difference between "false" and "true" righteousness. The Pharisees' righteousness was false. It was external, partial (Matt. 23:23), twisted, and self-centered. But God's righteousness is true. God's righteousness is inward, perfect, and a gift. When a person trusts Christ as Savior, Jesus' perfect sacrifice for sin is applied to his/her sin and God accounts Jesus' perfect righteousness to their life. It's a great trade.

We cannot keep the Law for salvation. But neither are we exempt from keeping the Law. We are to keep the Law, inside and out.

CHAPTER ELEVEN:

DON'T HURT PEOPLE

A POPULAR TV SERIES is "Making a Murderer." If you haven't seen it, it's a true documentary about Steven Avery, who served 18 years for attempted murder, then was exonerated. But two years later, he was arrested again for another murder. The story has been surrounded by controversy.

Murder is a popular subject. There are many TV shows and movies that describe murder and violence. Murder is often the one crime that casts a negative shadow on a city or community.

I think murder may be the most universally acknowledged sin in the world. Nobody likes a murderer. It's easy to hate a murderer like Adolph Hitler or Ted Bundy. But can we recognize a murderer in the mirror?

"Ye have heard that it was said of them of old time, Thou shalt not kill; and whosoever shall kill shall be in danger of the judgment." (Matthew 5:21)

The prohibition not to murder was God's idea from the beginning. Why is murder wrong? Because people are made in the image of God. To take a life is to disrespect the God in whose image it is made.

"Whoso sheddeth man's blood, by man shall his blood be shed: for in the image of God made he man." (Genesis 9:6)

Many people commend themselves for not committing murder. Obviously, if you have never taken a life you cannot be guilty of murder. Right? Not necessarily so. Jesus gets down to the root of the murder issue. Jesus reveals other actions that are considered murder.

1. Anger

"But I say unto you, That whosoever is angry with his brother without a cause shall be in danger of the judgment: and whosoever shall say to his brother, Raca, shall be in danger of the council: but whosoever shall say, Thou fool, shall be in danger of hell fire." (Matthew 5:22)

Jesus mentions something that we all are guilty of — anger. But not all anger is sinful. Jesus got angry when the crowd tried to prevent a man from being healed: *"And when he [Jesus] looked round about on them with anger, being grieved for the hardness of their hearts, he saith unto the man, Stretch forth thine hand. And he stretched it out: and his hand was restored whole as the other. " (Mark 3:5).* God is angry at the wicked: *"God judgeth the righteous, and God is angry with the wicked every day." (Psalm 7:11).* So, the anger Jesus is talking about must be beyond a righteous anger.

The anger that Jesus describes is a deep-seated, selfish anger. The Greek word Jesus uses (orgizo) means a brooding, simmering anger. I think of it as a grudge or long-held anger against someone. Do you hold a grudge against someone or can't stand to even think about someone? In Jesus' estimation, this is equal to murder because it is the same root sin that leads to murder.

2. Slander

Jesus talks about name-calling. He mentions calling someone "Raca." This Greek word, "raca," means empty-head, airhead, idiot, dummy. I think most of us use name-calling as a way of letting off frustration and anger to someone. It is a means of putting someone down. Jesus calls it murder.

It is popular to call people names. In sports, we call it "trash talk." Even though it seems like "everybody" is using this form of "murder," it should be removed from the life of a follower of Jesus. To call someone a name reflects on the One who made him or her. Do you call people names or put down someone with your words? In Jesus' teaching, it is equal to murder because the same desire to name-call is the same desire that leads to murder.

3. Condemnation

Jesus mentions calling someone a "Fool." For us, a fool is someone foolish. But in Biblical times, a fool had a different connotation. "Fool" is translation from the Greek word, moros. It is where we get the English word "moron." In Greek, it is especially used of one who is foolish in the moral issues of life.

It the Old Testament, a well-known passage says, *"The fool hath said in his heart, 'There is no God.'" (Psalm 14:1).* This term "fool" is not talking about intellectual deficiency, but moral and spiritual deficiency. A fool is someone who has a disregard for God. To call someone a fool, without just cause, is to pass judgment on their moral and spiritual understanding. We need to be careful about making moral judgments against people. Jesus will deal with this further (Matthew 7:1), but it does not mean we cannot call someone a "fool," because God and Jesus did. It simply means not to make quick moral evaluations of people based on our perception of them. We can judge actions and words, but only God can judge motive and desires.

I have known people who have attempted to assign people to eternal Hell. We do not have that authority nor have that kind of knowledge. Only God knows the spiritual life and motives of a person. Even if a person lived like the devil all their life, who knows but they may have repented just prior to their death.

The action of the thief on the cross reminds us never to judge someone (Luke 23:33-43). The man was a guilty robber. If someone did not hear his plea to Jesus of "Lord, remember me" and Jesus' reply 'Today, thou shalt be in Paradise,' they would have placed him in Hell because of his sin. But at the last moment, he turned to Christ. When I do funerals, even if the person has made no public profession of faith, I will leave their eternal destiny to God. I am not their judge. All I know is that every person will one day face God. And I know that God is a loving and merciful God. I hope that they turned in repentance to Jesus as Savior before they meet Him as Judge.

Do you make moral judgments about someone based on your limited knowledge? If so, you may be guilty of murder. This is the most serious, because this is dealing with moral and spiritual issues.

Who isn't guilty of anger, slander, or condemnation? Jesus has just condemned me of murder (killing) because I will admit I am guilty of anger, slander, and condemnation of others. I didn't physically kill anyone, but the same emotions and attitudes that lead to murder are the same that lead to anger, slander, and condemnation. Jesus is dealing with our heart. We may not have killed someone, but we probably have destroyed their spirit, soul, and reputation.

As much as the sins of anger and hatred impact our relationship with others, they also affect our relationship to God.

*"Therefore if thou bring thy gift to the altar, and there re-
memberest that thy brother hath ought against thee; Leave
there thy gift before the altar, and go thy way; first be rec-
onciled to thy brother, and then come and offer thy gift."
(Matthew 5:23-24)*

What is more important than our worship of God? You'll
find out. Jesus commanded us to interrupt our worship of
God with something else. Christians like to discuss what
makes worship meaningful. Christians fight over the right
kind of atmosphere, songs, and environment that make
worship meaningful. Worship is not enhanced by music,
prayers, architecture, or preaching as much as better relationships between those who go to church.

First things first! What is most important, our relationship
with God or with others? Obviously, our relationship with
God is primary. Jesus told us to *"Seek first the kingdom
of God" (Matthew 6:33).* But before you can have a good
experience with God, you must settle the problem between
you and your "brother." If you have not attempted to make
peace with others, you will find it difficult to find peace
with God.

As a guilty murderer, we need the forgiveness of God. Just
as Jesus forgave the thief beside Him on the cross, He will
forgive you and save your soul. Now, go and sin no more.
Treat others with kindness. Pray for your enemies and do
them good. And by all means, treat others better than yourself. Treat them like Jesus.

CHAPTER TWELVE:

KEEP YOUR MARRIAGE COMMITMENT

A DULTERY! WHAT A nasty word! It's no wonder people don't call it that. Adultery is often referred to as an affair, a fling, illicit love, even an extramarital relationship — anything but adultery. It seems every time I turn around, people are unfaithful to their wedding vows and destroy their marriage.

It is no surprise that one of God's Ten Commandments is: Thou shalt not commit adultery. Adultery destroys marriages, families, and individuals. But in the Sermon on the Mount, Jesus goes beyond the act of adultery. He encourages those who follow Him to have a much higher calling than to simply obey the law.

"Ye have heard that it was said by them of old time, Thou shalt not commit adultery: But I say unto you, That whosoever looketh on a woman to lust after her hath committed adultery with her already in his heart. And if thy right eye offend thee, pluck it out, and cast it from thee: for it is profitable for thee that one of thy members should perish, and not that thy whole body should be cast into hell. And if thy right hand offend thee, cut it off, and cast it from thee: for it is profitable for thee that one of thy members should perish, and not that thy whole body should be cast into hell." (Matthew 5:27-30)

The Desire for Adultery

Jesus tells us that "looking" with lust is adultery of the heart. This "looking" is not just a passing glance. In our society, immodesty abounds and it is near impossible not to see something that might be inappropriate. But Jesus is talking about an intentional look with the purpose of lusting. I've often counseled young men that it's not the first look that's wrong. It's the second. Martin Luther said, "You can't keep a bird from flying over your head, but you can keep him from building a nest in your hair."

Jesus is dealing with the heart. If you have a heart that wants to lust, you will find something to look at. And some people think that, as long as one does not commit adultery, it is okay to look. I've heard the excuse given for lusting as, "Just because you are on a diet doesn't mean you can't look at the menu."

Please notice that the look does not cause a man to commit adultery in his heart. He already has committed adultery. Lustful looking does not cause sin; sin causes lustful looking. Again, Jesus goes beyond the act to the heart.

We live in a world filled with lust. One marketing strategy is: Sex Sells. The porn industry generates $13 billion each year in the U.S. Internet porn alone is a $3 billion-per-year business. One statistic that surprised me is: 67 percent of young men and 49 percent of young women say viewing porn is an acceptable way to express one's sexuality. However, 68 percent of divorce cases involved one party meeting a new lover through the Internet. About 56 percent of divorce cases involved one party having an obsessive interest in pornographic websites. Those who have ever committed adultery are 218 percent more likely to have looked at porn.

Women are not exempt. Arthur Pink said, "If lustful looking is so grievous a sin, then those who dress and expose themselves with the desire to be looked at and lusted after... are not less but perhaps more guilty." It is one thing to look attractive; another to look seductive.

Adultery and lust are based on God-given desires and appetites. It is God who created sexual desire and allowed the sexual experience to be enjoyable. However, for our protection, He confined our sexual intimacy within the bounds of a committed marriage. Sex is so valuable to God that He wants it protected. Yet, it is so powerful that it often breaks those bounds and creates destruction and broken relationships everywhere.

The Deliverance

Lust can enslave its victims. Any sin can become a habit. The result of sin is always death. Jesus not only helps us understand the subtle temptation of adultery and lust, He also helps us have the victory.

Jesus warns of anything that would cause a person to "stumble." In other words, if there is something in your life that is causing you to do something wrong, you need to deal with it. The Greek word He used is skandalizo. It means "to cause to fall" — much like bait in a trap. Anything that causes us to fall into sin should be eliminated. Jesus says to cut it out of our life.

Jesus says if our eye or hand causes us to sin, we should remove it. Lust is a problem of the heart. So, what good would plucking out an eye or cutting off our hand do? Cutting off body parts does not eliminate sin. If sin is a matter of the heart, there is nothing we can do with our body that will prevent it. Jesus is not referring to a physical cutting off. Jesus' point is that we should give up whatever is necessary to protect us from evil. It is better to not experience some things this life offers in order to enter a life, which is life indeed.

So, what are some practical steps to fighting lust? According to Covenant Eyes, we find 3 Biblical strategies for fighting lust. These are based on 2 Timothy 2:22: *"Flee also youthful lusts; but pursue righteousness, faith, love, peace with those who call on the Lord out of a pure heart."*

1. **Run From** (*"flee youthful lusts"*). Even though Christians have the Holy Spirit, we still live in a body that wants to lust. When you sense the urge to lust, run mentally (bounce your thoughts away from lustful imaginations), run visually (bounce your eyes away from lustful images), and run physically (walk or run from tempting situations). When Joseph was tempted to commit adultery with his master's wife, he ran away. He left his coat, but he kept his character.

2. **Run To** (*"pursue righteousness, faith, love, and peace"*). Run toward a new passion — becoming Christ-like. In the end, we all do what we really want to do. Some people become trapped by sin. But it is because they wanted to get close to it. We need to develop a strong desire for personal holiness and purity. Work on your relationship with Jesus Christ. Stay in His Word and pray.

3. **Run With** (*"along with those who call on the Lord from a pure heart."*). Run with brothers and sisters with the same vision. We must all find Christians who share our faith and convictions and will help us in our common struggle for holiness. If you do not have a Christian friend with whom you can share your burdens and struggles, you need to find one. Better than that, be a friend and help others remain pure.

If you decide to remain morally pure and decide to live a life of holiness, you will be in the minority. But the company you keep will make up for the few you keep with. Stay strong.

CHAPTER THIRTEEN:

BE HONEST

I N AN ELECTION year, we hear a lot of promises. Every politician promises what he or she will do when they get in office. But I will admit it is sometimes difficult to know whom to trust. Very few politicians have the integrity of Abraham Lincoln. They called him, "Honest Abe." It was Benjamin Franklin who first wrote, "Honesty is the best policy."

Truth is an honored characteristic and is required for justice. In a court, people must "swear to tell the truth, the whole truth, and nothing but the truth. So help me, God." Even gangs of criminals that use lying and cheating as part of their trade still demand truth among themselves.

"There is nothing as powerful as truth and often nothing as strange." — Daniel Webster

Jesus dealt with truth and falsehood in the Sermon on the Mount.

"Again, ye have heard that it hath been said by them of old time, Thou shalt not forswear thyself, but shalt perform unto the Lord thine oaths: But I say unto you, Swear not at all; neither by heaven; for it is God's throne: Nor by the earth; for it is his footstool: neither by Jerusalem; for it is the city of the great King. Neither shalt thou swear by thy head, because thou canst not make one hair white or black. But let your communication be, Yea, yea; Nay, nay: for whatsoever is more than these cometh of evil." (Matthew 5:33-37)

Though this is not an exact quotation of any one law of Moses, it is a summary of ideas based on three Old Testament passages recorded by Moses.

"And ye shall not swear by my name falsely, neither shalt thou profane the name of thy God: I am the Lord." (Leviticus 19:12)

"If a man vow a vow unto the Lord, or swear an oath to bind his soul with a bond; he shall not break his word, he shall do according to all that proceedeth out of his mouth." (Numbers 30:2)

"When thou shalt vow a vow unto the Lord thy God, thou shalt not slack to pay it: for the Lord thy God will surely require it of thee; and it would be sin in thee." (Deuteronomy 23:21)

Some people are confused about Jesus' statement about swearing. They think that swearing is prohibited. However, God allowed making an oath by His name (Lev. 19:12). He even commanded it in certain situations (Deut. 10:20; Jer. 12:16-17). So, Jesus is not condemning all sworn oaths.

We discover that many Old Testament saints made oaths. Abraham made an oath following a battle (Gen. 14:22-24). Jacob made an oath with his father-in-law (Gen 31:44-53). David and Jonathan, King Saul's son, made an oath (1 Sam. 20:16). The Apostle Paul made several oaths to back up the truthfulness of what he was writing or saying. (Rom. 1:9; 2 Cor. 1:23; Phil. 1:8; 1 Thess. 2:5,10).

God even made oaths. He made an oath to never destroy the earth by a flood (Gen. 9:9-10). He made an oath to send a Redeemer (Luke. 1:68, 73). He made an oath to raise His Son from the dead (Ps. 16:10). He made an oath to preserve and bless Israel (Is. 49:15-18). Jesus answered Caiaphas under oath that He was the Messiah, the Son of God (Matt. 26:63-64).

It appears God allows swearing an oath for a couple of reasons:

1. An oath is a sign of our allegiance to God rather than idols (Deut. 6:13; 10:20). God encouraged the people of Israel to make a public statement of their full devotion to Him as their God.

2. An oath is an accommodation to sinful nature. People lie. Our inclination to lie causes distrust among

people. In serious situations, an oath is permissible to give greater motivation to tell the truth. There is nothing Biblically wrong in placing your hand on a Bible in a court of law and swearing to tell the truth, as long as you tell the truth.

However, the religious leaders of Jesus' day were abusing oaths. Some were taking an oath that was neither necessary nor proper in the name of the Lord. They would swear by the name of the Lord in matters that were very small. Using God's name in an oath was unnecessary. No one ought to voluntarily take an oath unless it is a matter of controversy and the contention can't be settled any other way (Hebrews 6:16). You don't need to swear. Your word should be good enough.

Some were not swearing in the name of the Lord because they didn't want to keep it. In the Bible, people could swear by their own life (1 Sam. 1:26), their health (Ps. 15:4), the king (1 Sam. 17:55), their head, earth, heaven, the Temple, and Jerusalem (Matt. 5:34-36). All these were important, but people often felt that unless an oath was made with God's name, it was not as binding. But Jesus emphasized God's premium on truth in every situation. It does not matter whether you use an oath or not; you should always tell the truth.

I have discovered some principles and practices that help me understand the importance of always telling the truth.

1.   God's standard is absolute truth (Psalm 51:6; Prov. 6:16-17; 12:22; Ps. 119:163; 58:3-4; Jer. 9:3; Rev. 21:8;

James 5:12). Whenever the truth is profaned, God's name is profaned. Every lie is against God, regardless of the formula used. A half-truth is still a whole lie and a white lie is really black. An oath, no matter how strong the words used, is only as reliable as the one making it.

2. Life cannot be divided into compartments in which God is and is not involved. There is no church language and work language, church conduct and school conduct. Christianity is a religion that honors the common things. If it is something you would not tell God because it is not totally honest, it is something you shouldn't tell anybody else.

3. Use oaths sparingly. The Hebrew word shebuah, "swear," is in the passive voice and indicates we should be passive in swearing. This means it is good to only swear when called on to do so. Arthur Pink helps us understand this when he says, "When matters of controversy in men affect peace in society in general or particular and the peace depends on the right determination of them, it is okay for a believer to confirm the truth by invoking God, with the design to end the strife."

4. Honest people do not need to resort to oaths. Many people who have lost the trust of friends, family, and society must resort to oaths because their word is called into question. Christians should say what they mean and mean what they say. Let your "Yes" be "Yes" and your "No" be "No."

5. Control your tongue. Our speech often gets us into trouble. Since what you say is a result of what you think and believe, tongue control is achieved only when heart and mind are controlled (Matt. 12:34). Individually, people are inclined to truth only when it benefits them. We should be truthful because Jesus lives and controls our lives.

I often have told my children that, when you lie, you often need to tell another lie to cover it up. Then you have to remember all the lies you have told and to whom you have told them so you do not get into further trouble. The best course of action is to always tell the truth. God expects it. People deserve it. And you will feel good about yourself for it.

CHAPTER FOURTEEN:

TURN THE OTHER CHEEK

"TURN THE OTHER cheek." We've all heard, and often said, these words. They are spoken when a person hurts another person. Though it may be physical, often the hurts are emotional or social. I deal with a lot of people who have been hurt by others. This simple response is not so simple. It is hard to obey and hard to understand. How should we respond to evil?

Retaliation is an extension of our selfishness. It is natural to have a concern for our own protection. But concern for our own rights comes from selfishness. I'm not saying there isn't a time, place or situation when we should not protect ourselves. But the desire to seek revenge or retaliation stems from our selfishness and leads to lawlessness.

It is not possible for everyone to have everything they want. Whenever someone wins, someone often loses. So not everyone can have it all. Though we may attempt to be fair, life just isn't fair. To insist on our own way invariably tramples on the rights and welfare of others.

"You have heard that it was said, 'Eye for eye, and tooth for tooth.' But I tell you, do not resist an evil person." (Matthew 5:38-39a).

These words by Jesus have been misinterpreted to mean that Christians are to be doormats. It has been used to promote pacifism, conscientious objection to military service, lawlessness, and even anarchy.

So, what did Jesus mean?

"Eye for eye" is a quote from the Old Testament (Exodus 21:24). Simply put, it required that punishment match the crime. It had two purposes: (1) If obeyed, it would curtail further crime. (2) If administered, it would prevent excessive punishment based on personal vengeance. We are tempted to get more than just even.

But during Jesus' day, the religious leaders took this idea to a different application. Instead of acknowledging it as a limit on punishment, they used it as a mandate for vengeance. This principle was leveraged to demand that hurt be ministered to others. But Jesus' contemporaries did not just administer this within the judicial system. This principle was extended from law courts to personal relationships. If someone hurt you, you had the right to hurt him or her. This was an encouragement to personal vengeance and retaliation.

But Jesus turns it. His "resist not" forbids retaliation in personal relationships. Jesus did not mean we are not to be against evil. Certainly, Jesus fought evil in all its forms. And it doesn't mean government is not to punish evil. One of the government's God-given responsibilities is to punish evil (Romans 13:4). But rather than give evil for evil, we are to overcome someone's evil toward us by doing good to them (Rom. 12:21).

Jesus illustrated this principle with four basic human rights.

1. Dignity — 'Turn the other cheek'

"But I say unto you, That ye resist not evil: but whosoever shall smite thee on thy right cheek, turn to him the other also." (Matthew 5:39)

Because every person is created in God's image, Jesus demands that we treat one another with respect. But He knows that we will not always be so treated. People do not consistently treat one another with dignity. So how do we respond to humiliation?

A slap on the face was a demeaning act. To strike in another place, such as the head or stomach, may cause more harm. But a slap in the face on the cheek attacks one's honor. To slap on the "right" cheek indicates slapping with the back of the hand. Most people are right handed and to hit some-one with your right hand on the right cheek indicates a backward hit. It is not the force of the strike that hurts as much as the demeaning attitude. It comes from someone who seeks to humiliate us.

But even if we take this at face value, others hurt us, physi-cally or emotionally. How do we react? Naturally, we want to strike back. But how should we react? Jesus' point per-tains more to what we are not to do than what to do.

We are to turn the other cheek. This means we are not to offer further hurt. Turning the other cheek symbolizes non-retaliation. When we retaliate, it places the other per-son in a position to strike us back. This leads to an escala-tion in the confrontation. But when we decide not to fight back, it stops the spread of violence. Often, because it is so unnatural, it causes the person to consider what they have done and feel remorse. The situation has been calmed.

2. Security — 'Give your coat'

"And if any man will sue thee at the law, and take away thy coat, let him have thy cloke also." (Matthew 5:40).

Jesus tells us that if someone wants take our coat, we should give it to him. Not only the coat, but give him our cloak (cloke). These two words are interesting. The term "coat" referred to something like a shirt and the "cloke" was an outer garment, similar to our jacket or overcoat. So, Jesus is encouraging us to give more than is expected.

Sometimes in a Jewish court case, a fine could be paid in something other than money. If a person did not have the money, they could give an item of clothing. The outer garment, a cloke, however, was required to be returned (Ex. 22:26-27). The cloke was not only the outer garment; for the poor, it often was a bed and covering. It served as protection against the weather.

Jesus says to give the coat and cloke. We are to give more than is expected. We should be willing to surrender even a cloke, rather than cause offense or hard feelings with our adversary.

3. Liberty — 'Go the extra mile'

"And whosoever shall compel thee to go a mile, go with him twain." (Matthew 5:41).

Freedom is important. But freedom is not to be cherished and protected at the expense of righteousness or being a faithful witness. Our personal liberties are not as important as our personal relationships.

The Jews hated the Roman occupation, especially the military. A Roman soldier could legally force a civilian to carry his pack for one mile. Anywhere and anytime needed, the Jew had to obey. But Jesus says to carry the pack a second mile.

This is one of those clichés that most do not realize comes from the Bible. To "go the extra mile" is used to describe situations where we go beyond what is expected of us. It means to give a little extra. Jesus not only encourages us to be involved in any form of service others demand of us, He encourages us to volunteer to do more.

4. Prosperity — 'Give to those who ask'

"Give to him that asketh thee, and from him that would borrow of thee turn not thou away." (Matthew 5:42).

We are not required to respond to every foolish, selfish request. Sometimes to give a person what he wants does more harm than good. But we should offer to give what is needed as soon as we know the need, whether asked or not.

Gandhi (reformer of India) led India into freedom from England and used the Sermon on the Mount as his inspiration. Rather than civil disobedience, he used truth to change his country. He said "an eye for an eye only makes the whole world blind."

Martin Luther King, Jr. in a sermon based on Matthew 5:43-45 said, "Love is the only force capable of transforming an enemy into a friend for it has creative and redemptive power." He went on to apply his theme to the racial crisis in the United States. King was determined to "meet hate with love." We would do well to follow this principle.

CHAPTER FIFTEEN:

BE NICE TO MEAN PEOPLE

Do you remember that "friend" who made fun of you the first day you wore your glasses in elementary school? I do. When I was in 5th grade, I got glasses for the first time. They were those bulky frames that were as big as half your face. My friends called me "Eagle Eye." It was one of the worst days of my life.

But it is not just children who can say bad things about you. I have watched arguments played out on Facebook between two people. Some of the things people say about each other can be as unkind as a junior high prank.

Most of us have been hurt badly by someone else. Do you remember the hurt you felt when your heart was crushed when someone you loved betrayed you? The world is filled with people who are basically unkind.

Some people can just be mean. They don't like us. And we don't like them much either. But, as a Christian, we are supposed to have a better attitude toward them. Jesus tells us we are to love our enemies.

"Ye have heard that it hath been said, Thou shalt love thy neighbor, and hate thine enemy. But I say unto you, Love your enemies, bless them that curse you, do good to them that hate you, and pray for them which despitefully use you, and persecute you; That ye may be the children of your Father which is in heaven: for he makes his sun to rise on the evil and on the good, and sends rain on the just and on the unjust. For if ye love them which love you, what reward have ye? do not even the publicans the same? And if ye salute your brethren only, what do ye more than others? do not even the publicans so? Be ye therefore perfect, even as your Father which is in heaven is perfect." (Matthew 5:43-48)

If anybody knew about enemies, it was Jesus. All through His ministry, He had people who tried to discount Him and destroy Him. He would one day be betrayed, beaten, crucified, and killed by His enemies. So how does Jesus say we should treat our enemies? He tells us simply to love them.

Love is often used as an emotional word. When we think of love we think of this wonderful, positive feeling we have for others. But that is not what we gather from Jesus. Jesus tells us to love and then gives us three practical actions. Love is an action word. What are three actions we should do for our enemies?

First, Jesus says to "Bless your Enemies." Mean people are mean with their mouth. They say mean things. But as Christians, we have to be conscious of what comes from our mouth. When a person insults us, we aren't to insult them back. Instead, we are to respond by blessing them. In doing this, we also receive a blessing.

How do we bless those who speak evil toward us? We must bless them by speaking well of them. Behind our backs, mean people tear us down. But behind their backs, we should speak kind words about them. Kindness is the ability to love people more than they really deserve.

Second, Jesus says to "Do Good to your Enemies." Love is an action verb. Love and hate do not necessarily have to do with our emotions. Love's question is never who to love, but how to love.

This is the positive side of "turn the other cheek." When we turn the other cheek, it speaks of what we do not do. But when we do good for them, this is a positive response to evil. We don't retaliate. We show love. Find an opportunity to do good to those who hate you.

Third, Jesus says to "Pray for your Enemies." It is hard to love our enemies. It is not natural. But praying for them helps. It not only helps them, but it helps us. It helps us not to have an angry, bitter spirit toward them. Dietrich Bonheoffer, a pastor killed in Nazi Germany, said, "This is the supreme demand. Through the medium of prayer we go to our enemy, stand by his side, and plead for him to God."

Praying for my enemies has been one of the best strategies I have found to help my own attitude. Bitterness doesn't hurt my enemies as much as it hurts me. So, if I notice a bitter, angry attitude growing toward someone, I put that person on my "Enemy List" and pray for them daily. And soon, they are no longer an enemy.

It is hard to know what to pray for our enemies. We want to pray that God takes revenge against them for us. And sometimes that happens. David often prayed like this. But I have left my prayers to three simple requests: (1) May they do God's will; (2) May God's will be done for them; (3) May God bless them. I leave the results up to God.

When we treat our enemies with love, we show that we are God's children. Loving enemies doesn't make us children of God, but proves we are children of God.

One of the criticisms of Christianity is it doesn't live up to its faith. People know enough about the Bible and Christ's teaching to know that we don't live as He lived. Ask just about anybody what the central teaching of Christianity is, and most will say something about loving others. Even non-believers understand that Christianity is a religion of love.

But even a person who has never heard of Christ or the teachings of Christianity would wonder at a person who loves his enemies. Loving our enemies — it is so uncharacteristic of human nature that people will take notice. They may think you are unconventional or even crazy, but they will notice. They may not like it, but they will have a certain amount of respect for you.

Those who claim to follow Christ are to have a higher standard of love than the rest of the world. Often people say, "You do me bad, so I'll do you bad.' Or, "You do me good, then I'll do you good." "You scratch my back and I'll scratch yours. Then we'll call it quits."

But loving others, especially when they don't deserve it, is the kind of love that our Heavenly Father expresses. We are more like God when we forgive and love others than just about anything else we can do.

CHAPTER SIXTEEN:

GIVE ALL YOU CAN

A S A PASTOR, I have been careful how I teach on money. Money is a very personal matter. But Jesus teaches that "where your treasure is, there will your heart be also." Our hearts are tied to our money.

Because money is tied to our hearts, it comes as no surprise that money can be a sensitive subject. Money has gotten many religious leaders in trouble. One of the requirements for a pastor is the freedom from greed (1 Timothy 3:3). Yet, many ministries and church leaders have used their church leadership position for personal wealth. I think this may be one reason Jesus talks about money. He wants to make sure we have a good understanding of the correct way to use it.

The only time Jesus asked for money was when he wanted to use a coin as an object lesson. He borrowed a coin to show that Caesar's name and image was on it. He then presented his famous commentary on the separation of government and religion, *"Give that which is Caesar's to Caesar, and give to God what is God's." (Mark 12:13-17).*

In the Sermon on the Mount Jesus talks extensively about money and the stress and worry it causes (Mathew 6:19-34). However, he opens Matthew 6 with a discussion about giving to others in need.

This begins a section on outward religion. Giving is our religion toward others (Matthew 6:1-4). Praying is our religion toward God (Matthew 6:5-15). Fasting is our religion toward ourself (Matthew 6:16-18).

Note: I use "religion" for our works for God. In Matthew 5, we discover Jesus' teachings about some of the activities we are not to do (murder, adultery, etc.). In Matthew 6, we discover Jesus' teachings about some of the activities we are to do (giving, praying, fasting).

False Giving

Take heed that ye do not your alms before men, to be seen of them: otherwise ye have no reward of your Father which is in heaven. Therefore when thou doest thine alms, do not sound a trumpet before thee, as the hypocrites do in the synagogues and in the streets, that they may have glory of men. Verily I say unto you, They have their reward." (Matthew 6:1-2)

People were giving to the poor so others would notice them. Jesus calls a person who gives so others will notice a "hypocrite." In Jesus' day, a "hypocrite" was an actor who wore a mask of the individual he was portraying. For example, if the actor's character was sad, he would wear a frown on his mask; if the character was happy, he would wear a mask with a smile on it. The word "hypocrite" soon came to mean "laying aside your true identity and assume a false one."

In a play, deceit is an accepted fact. We know actors are not themselves, but playing a part. But in life, hypocrisy is a deliberate attempt to deceive people.

The Greek word Jesus uses for "to be noticed" is theomai and ironically it is related to our word "theatre." Jesus is warning about practicing a form of righteousness whose purpose is to show off before men.

Christians are enticed with many pleas to help the poor and hurting. It seems every day I receive a phone call to help a good organization that is helping people in need. It is easy to appeal to our emotions with sad pictures or heart-wrenching stories. My heart is often touched with the need.

Other ministries appeal to our pride and love for recognition to bring in money. It boosts our ego to see our name as subscribers to charities and a supporter of good causes. It is just as wrong to appeal to wrong motives to give, as it is to have wrong motives to give. Be careful of your motives for giving to good causes.

True Giving

"But when thou doest alms, let not thy left hand know what thy right hand doeth: That thine alms may be in secret: and thy Father which seeth in secret himself shall reward thee openly." (Matthew 6:3-4)

Rather than give so others will notice, Jesus appeals to a greater audience — God. Jesus reminds us that our giving to others in need will be noticed. But our reward will be in proportion to whom we wanted to notice our giving.

- **Give Dutifully**. Jesus did not say "if" you give, but "when" you give. I think one of the reasons God allows some to have more is so they can have more to give to those who have less. The poor are a test of our Christianity. Will we give to help meet their needs?

- **Give Secretly.** Jesus makes a confusing appeal. We are not to let one hand know what the other is giving. While our hands do not think independently of our brain, let alone each other, I think Jesus emphasizes the secrecy of our giving. Not only are you not to tell others of your giving, don't tell yourself. The question is not what the hand is doing, but what the heart is thinking. The most satisfying giving and the giving that God blesses is that which is done and forgotten. It is done in love out of response to a need. When the need is met, the giver goes on, not wanting the recognition.

- **Give Hopefully.** When we give correctly, we have every reason to believe that God will reward our giving. But our reward is not always what we may think. Though the natural law of sowing and reaping would lead us to believe that, if we give financially, we will reap financially, this is not always the result. There are different ways God rewards. Often, the only reward genuine love wants when making a gift to the needy is to see that need relieved. When we give to feed the hungry, there are few greater rewards than to see someone eat a wonderful meal.

- **Give Lovingly.** Christians are bombarded by appeals for money. We are to give to our local church (1 Cor. 16:2). We are also to give to those in need when we have opportunity and ability. These gifts are given as to God. God, however, does not need our gifts, because He is entirely sufficient in Himself. The need is on our part and those we serve in His name (Phil. 4:7). The poor are giving us a gift by being the recipient of our gracious gift. We are more like God when we give than when we receive.

Giving is part of God's cycle of blessing (Prov. 11:25). As we give, God blesses. He finds in every giver a channel through which He can send His gifts. As God blesses us, we give out of what He has given us. The more He gives, the more He wants us to give. There is an endless supply (Philippians 4:19).

In John MacArthur's commentary on Matthew 1-7, he presents some guidelines for Christian giving. I share those with you to help you be a better giver.

7 Principles to guide us in non-hypocritical giving

1. Giving from the heart is investing with God (Luke 6:38).

2. Genuine giving is to be sacrificial (2 Sam. 24:24; Mark 12:41-44).

3. Giving has no relationship to how much a person has (Luke 16:10).

4. Material giving correlates to spiritual blessings (Luke 16:11-12).

5. Giving is to be personally determined (2 Cor. 9:7).

6. We are to give in response to needs. We are to determine if and when real needs exist before giving money (2 Thess. 3:10).

7. Giving demonstrates love, not law. The New Testament has no commands for amount or percentage of giving. The amount is determined by the love of our own hearts and the needs of others.

The heart is the key to giving. If our heart is right with God, what we give will be rewarded. We should give without expecting anything in return. If we remember, God will forget. But if we forget, God will remember. Meet those in need around you and leave the bookkeeping to God (Luke 17:10).

"From what we get, we can make a living; what we give, however, makes a life." – Arthur Ashe

CHAPTER SEVENTEEN:

PRAY TO GOD

WHAT DO YOU think about prayer? Some think God works His will regardless of the way, or even if, people pray. They think prayer is simply lining up with what God is going to do anyway. Some believe God's actions are determined based on our prayers. Prayer, to them, is asking God to do what He otherwise would not do. Scripture supports a balance of both views.

So how does prayer really work? How can we know if God really hears our prayers? Understanding what makes prayer work is not required, nor is it completely possible. Much like our cell phones or computers, it's nice and often helpful to know how they work, but not vital to gain help from them. Regardless, I encourage you to pray.

Jesus spent quite a bit of time talking about prayer in His Sermon on the Mount. He helps us understand how to pray so God will hear us.

The Wrong Audience – People

"And when thou prayest, thou shalt not be as the hypocrites are: for they love to pray standing in the synagogues and in the corners of the streets, that they may be seen of men. Verily I say unto you, They have their reward." (Matthew 6:5)

If you want to talk with someone, you had better make sure you are talking with him or her. There have been times when I have emailed someone, but I had the wrong contact number. It can be embarrassing. But even more important, you had better make sure that, if you think you are talking with God, you really are.

Jesus warns that some people pray so others can notice their praying. The primary audience is not God, but those who hear the prayer. This reminds me of a time when a child was learning to say "grace" before a meal and was rather quiet. When the father raised the objection that he couldn't hear him, the little child replied, "I wasn't talking to you." Though others may hear our prayer, we need to make sure our primary audience is God.

The Jews ritually prayed "The Shema" (from Deut. 6 & Num. 5) three times a day. At the appointed times (9a.m., Noon & 3 a.m.) they knelt to pray toward the Temple. Evidently, some of the religious leaders made sure they were in a prominent place at the appointed time so others could see them. They wanted to be seen and heard by other people. They got what they wanted, but God did not listen.

I have often found that God gives you what you really want. If you pray for mainly the benefit of yourself or others, you got it. But if you really want God to listen to you, He will hear not only your words but also your heart. He even hears our heart when we cannot put our prayer into words.

The Right Audience – God

"But thou, when thou prayest, enter into thy closet, and when thou hast shut thy door, pray to thy Father which is in secret; and thy Father which seeth in secret shall reward thee openly." (Matthew 6:6)

Jesus knew what it was like to talk with God. His most intense times of spiritual opposition were when He spent time in prayer. For example, His temptation in the wilderness was a time for one-on-one battle with Satan Himself. Finally, in the Garden of Gethsemane, Jesus had a personal struggle with His Father's will. When He asked His disciples to pray, they fell asleep. Satan will do anything to keep people from talking with God.

A good definition of prayer is "communion of God." I simply tell new Christians, "If you can talk, you can talk with God." If God is not involved, it is not prayer. The most important secret Jesus sees is not the words we say, but the thoughts of our hearts.

Rather than pray in public, Jesus encouraged prayer in private. I have found that it helps to have a quiet, private place of prayer and devotion. The desire to pray will create such a place. Jesus did this. He prayed in a garden, forest, mountain, and early in the morning.

Those who pray secretly will be rewarded openly. What reward can you expect from secret prayer? Secret prayer produces Christian character. This inward, humble character wins the admiration and confidence of others publicly.

Here's a great statement to consider: If you pray more in public than private, you are less interested in God's approval than human praise.

False Content – Meaningless Repetition

"But when ye pray, use not vain repetitions, as the heathen do: for they think that they shall be heard for their much speaking." (Matthew 6:7)

Jesus condemns "vain repetitions." The Greek word used is battalogeo and means idle, thoughtless chatter. It also means to say the same thing but in different words. We find an example of this among pagans in 1 Kings 18:26 when the priests of Baal cried, "O Baal, hear us" over and over all day. But nobody heard these repetitions.

Prayer that is thoughtless and indifferent is offensive to God. God desires prayers that not only grip our mind, but also our heart and emotions.

You should know that God does not forbid the repetition of genuine requests. One of Jesus' parables highlighted a widow's repeated requests for help as a model for our prayer (Luke 18:2-7). The Apostle Paul prayed three concentrated prayers for release from a *"thorn in the flesh"* (2 Corinthians 12:7-8). Even Jesus, prayed three times in the Garden of Gethsemane with *"the same words"* (Matthew 26:39-44). So, it's okay to repeat your prayers, like the Lord's Prayer, as long as it is not empty (vain).

Jesus is against prayer that is all words and no meaning, all lips and no head or heart. Not only must our hearts be right before God will hear our prayer, but also our minds.

True Content – Sincere Requests (Matthew 6:8)

"Be not ye therefore like unto them: for your Father knoweth what things ye have need of, before ye ask." (Matthew 6:8)

Marin Luther says, "By our praying… we are instructing ourselves more than we are him." God is not ignorant that we need to inform Him, nor is He stubborn that we need to persuade Him. We need to simply and sincerely ask Him. God is waiting to talk.

Why should we pray?

First, prayer helps us feel our need. It is one thing to be needy, but another to recognize and be so needy we need to ask. God requires a sense of need and dependence on Him. Prayer awakens that sense of need.

Second, prayer encourages our faith in God. I have found that the more I sincerely and honestly pray for something, the more I really believe that God can do what I request. Even if I pray for a long time for something, I will get to the place where I realize that God might not say yes to my request. But my faith has gotten stronger because I believe that if it doesn't happen, God has bigger plans for me. So, even if the answer to my prayer is "No" my faith is strengthened. I trust God.

Some Practical Suggestions for Prayer:

1. **Have a place.** It's good to have a familiar spot that is quiet and private. Jesus did not say when and where to pray because He wanted it to be voluntary. But He did want it to be private. To mandate when and where would lead to formality and limit true prayer.

   Have you ever noticed that if you have a chair that you consistently do a certain function (i.e. eat, study, nap, watch TV, read, etc.) it doesn't take long to get in the mood to do it? If you have a "prayer closet" you can get right into the action of prayer. In the recent movie, War Room, Miss Clara had a closet where she does her business with God. You need a place or chair.

2. **Be alone.** We should pray with others. But our power is when we are one-on-one with God.

I know for many, especially young moms and dads or college students, it is nearly impossible to have any time alone. You may need to be creative to find a private spot. You may not be able to have an extended time alone with God. But even a short prayer, like the Lord's Prayer, is sufficient.

You can be in a crowd and yet have a private time with God. It is good to be physically alone, but if not, talk privately with God. He hears your thoughts.

3. **Speak freely to God and cherish confidence in His presence.** God is not alarmed at your raw emotions. You can talk to Him about anything. If you are mad, He already knows that. If you are hurt, He has already felt your pain. You can expose your heart to Him and He will love you more than you've ever felt love.

Though you might not "feel" God is near, you can trust that He is. He said He would hear you. When you are alone, you are never alone. God hears your weakest cries. Just know that He is with you. As an old song reminds me, "when you can't see His hand, trust His heart."

CHAPTER EIGHTEEN:

PRAY LIKE JESUS

T HE LORD'S PRAYER is my favorite part of the Sermon on the Mount. It has become one of my daily spiritual disciplines. Every day I pray through the Lord's Prayer.

"After this manner therefore pray ye: Our Father which art in heaven, Hallowed be thy name. Thy kingdom come, Thy will be done in earth, as it is in heaven. Give us this day our daily bread. And forgive us our debts, as we forgive our debtors. And lead us not into temptation, but deliver us from evil: For thine is the kingdom, and the power, and the glory, forever. Amen." (Matthew 6:9-13)

Though we call this the Lord's Prayer, it is really the Disciple's Prayer. For example, Jesus never had to pray for forgiveness, but we do. Jesus gave this prayer as a guideline and as a recitation. He told us to pray like this prayer and He told us to pray this prayer (Luke 11:1-4).

Prayer is a powerful resource for every Christian. J. Edgar Hoover (former FBI Director) once said, "The spectacle of a nation praying is more awe-inspiring than the explosion of an atomic bomb. The force of prayer is greater than any possible combination of man-controlled powers, because prayer is man's greatest means of trapping the infinite resources of God."

Earlier, Jesus pointed out the fault in the prayers of many people. God does not hear the prayers of a religious hypocrite (Matthew 6:5). Nor does he hear the mechanical prayer of the pagan (Matthew 6:7). So, Jesus shows us how to pray the right way so God will hear.

What should we pray about?

1. God's Glory

In prayer, God's concerns are the first priority. Our own needs are second and are committed to Him.

- **His Name**

Because of Jesus, we can call God "Father." Though all people are God's creation (Malachi 2:10), not all are His children (John 1:12). Only salvation makes us a child of God. To "hallow" His name is to make it set apart, separate, and special. God's name is to be special.

- **His Kingdom**

    Jesus' kingdom will come at His second coming (Matt. 24:27). But His kingdom comes personally to people by conversion (Matt. 18:1-4) and by Christians living by His commands.

- **His Will**

    It is foolish to resist it, wisdom to discern it, and wise to do it. Though God is sovereign, it is clear that He also commands us to exercise our will according to His will. Pray that God's will becomes our own will. Pray that His will prevails on earth as it does in Heaven.

    When our life and prayers are self-centered, we are concerned with: 1: Our own name – embossed on letterhead, headlines in news, defending it when it is attacked. 2: Our own empire (kingdoms) – we are bossy, influencing and manipulating to boost our ego. 3: Our own will – always wanting our own way and getting upset when it is denied. But we should be concerned with God's name, God's kingdom, and God's will.

2. **People's Needs**

    Putting God first will not eliminate our needs. To not pray about them at all is as great an error as to allow them to dominate our prayers.

- **Daily Bread**

  "Daily Bread" is symbolic of our physical needs. It is not only a petition but also an affirmation that God takes care of us. We are to rely on the Lord one day at a time. God responds to our needs day by day.

- **Forgiveness**

  Our failures put us in God's "debt" since we owe Him complete obedience. Sin is a moral and spiritual debt to God that must be paid. Because sin is our greatest problem, our greatest need is forgiveness. This forgiveness is from a "Father" not a "Judge."

  We are to forgive because it is the character of righteousness. Forgiveness of others reflects God's own gracious forgiveness. It frees our conscience of guilt and benefits the whole family of believers. Forgiveness delivers us from God's discipline and brings God's forgiveness. The emphasis is that those who have received forgiveness will forgive others. This is not forgiveness for salvation, but forgiveness for fellowship.

- **Protection from Temptation**

  "Deliverance" and "Lead me not" is the negative and positive of the same request – to be free of evil. God will deliver us if we call on Him.

Real Forgiveness

I find it interesting that, as soon as Jesus finished His teaching on the Lord's Prayer, He went right back to one of the phrases of the prayer to emphasize and further explain it. The phrase "forgive us our debts as we forgive our debtors" needed further explanation.

"For if ye forgive men their trespasses, your heavenly Father will also forgive you: But if ye forgive not men their trespasses, neither will your Father forgive your trespasses." (Matthew 6:14-15)

By using the word "for" to begin this section, it is almost as if receiving and extending forgiveness is the highest priority of this prayer. It may be. David reminds us that if *"I regard iniquity in my heart, the Lord will not hear me." (Psalm 66:18)*. Forgiveness is key to prayer.

Some interpret this verse to mean that our eternal destiny is dependent on our forgiving other people. Our salvation is not dependent on anything we do or do not do. It is totally reliant on what Jesus has done on the cross.

But this verse does teach that our relationship with God will be affected when we refuse to forgive others. Our relationship with God is not independent of our relationship with others. I love what John reminds us. *"If a man say, I love God, and hateth his brother, he is a liar: for he that loveth not his brother whom he hath seen, how can he love God whom he hath not seen?" (1 John 4:10)*. If someone refuses to forgive others, they either do not understand God's forgiveness of their sin, or have never been forgiven at all and are not a Christian. When we refuse to forgive, we are behaving like an unbeliever.

As I finish up these thoughts on the Lord's Prayer, I want to be real practical. As mentioned earlier, I use this prayer as a guide to my own personal prayer. Sometimes this will take me five minutes. Other times I will spend nearly half an hour or more thinking through the topics in this prayer.

I want to share with you my outline as I pray. I am grateful to Bob Beltz and his wonderful book, Becoming a Man of Prayer, for giving me many of these ideas. I have made adjustments and changes as I have felt God move my heart. You will notice a general outline and topics. Use and adjust as God works in your heart to teach you to pray.

Getting Started — 'Father'

I address God the Father, Son, and Holy Spirit. Each has a unique relationship to me: Father (intimacy, sonship, love, fear), Son (Savior, Lord, Friend, Brother), Holy Spirit (ever-present, moving, powerful).

Getting Focused — 'Hallowed Be Thy Name'

I recognize the meaning of God's name. I personally affirm to God that He is my "I am" (always present, cause to be, I will be who I will be). Sometimes I use Jesus' "I am" statements (I am the Bread of Life, the Good Shepherd, the

Light of the World, etc.). I will take this time to thank Him for what He has done (I list 5 things every day).

Divine Intervention — 'Thy Kingdom Come'

I pray for Jesus' soon return and God's will to be done in my life, my family, my church, my friends, our nation, and the world. Every day I ask God's will be done, that each of these will do God's will, and that God will bless each, including myself. I ask a blessing on each of my family members. I also have a list of church members, friends, other pastors, missionaries, and others whom I pray for. That list has gotten quite large. So, I have divided each by last name and pray every day for a different name alphabetically. For example, on the first day of the month, I pray for all those whose last name ends in A.

Provision — 'Give Us This Day'

I pray for my daily needs. I pray for God's financial provision for my life (since that is how I get my bread). For me, this means I pray for my church since I get paid by my church. For some, you may need to pray for your business or company. I also commit to meet the conditions of God's financial provision: give/tithe to God's work, be generous to the poor, work hard, spend wisely, save, budget, etc.). I also talk to God about my tasks for the day, my desires, and any sources of anxiety I may have.

Forgiveness — 'Forgive Us Our Sins'

This is the time I confess my sin and my sins. I recognize that I am in constant need of God's grace and forgiveness. I need help transforming the defects of my character. I pray that the fruit of the Spirit would be evident in my life. I need strength to overcome my old nature issues (greed, lust, rage, laziness, selfishness, etc.). I pray for the Holy Spirit to search me and point out any areas that need confessing.

I also pray for forgiveness for others. Not knowing what the day will hold, I commit to treat any offenses against me with forgiveness and compassion. I ask to be reminded that bitterness doesn't hurt the other person as much as it hurts me. So, like Job (Job 42), I pray for my enemies every day. I currently have a list of five people that I ask God to help them do God's will, that God would do His will for them, and that God would bless them.

Protection — 'Deliver Us'

I pray for God's guidance in life. I don't want to be led into any trap. I pray for my own personal holiness. I also pray for protection and list each piece of the armor of God (Ephesians 6:10-18). I also admit my humbleness before God and try to humble myself. I ask to be delivered from any evil. So, I pray for a spiritual hedge of protection around my family and me from any evil. I also pray for freedom from any bondage of bad habits that I am susceptible to.

Affirmation — 'Thine is...'

Jesus finished His prayer with: *"Thine is the kingdom, and the power, and the glory, forever."* So, I always finish my prayer the same. It is God's kingdom, not mine. (Lord, let me live a kingdom life today). It is God's power (Lord, strengthen me with your power in my inner man.) It is God's glory (Lord, glorify Yourself through my life today. AMEN!

I heard a story that reminds me of the importance of prayer. Shortly after Dallas Theological Seminary was founded in 1924, it came to the point of bankruptcy. All creditors were going to foreclose at noon. In a prayer meeting with Dr. Chafer, Harry Ironside prayed, "Lord, You own cattle on a thousand hills. Could you sell some and send the money?" While praying, a tall Texan in cowboy boots went into the business office. "I just sold two carloads of cattle in Fort Worth. I've been trying to make a business deal, but it fell through. I feel compelled to give it to the seminary." The secretary took it to the office. Dr. Chafer took the check. It was exactly the amount of the debt. He turned to Ironside and said, "Harry, God sold the cattle!"

CHAPTER NINETEEN:

SAY NO TO YOURSELF

U P TO THIS point in Matthew 6, Jesus has dealt with two forms of religion, giving to the poor and prayer. He now is going to talk about fasting. Giving and prayer are what we do. But fasting emphasizes what we do not do.

Fasting is an exercise in self-denial and self-discipline to abstain from food. Going without food or drink for any period of time is a form of fasting. "Breakfast" means to "break a fast."

Many ancient pagans believed that demons could enter the body through food. When they felt they were under demonic attack, they would fast to prevent more evil spirits from gaining access to their bodies. In modern western society, fasting has become popular for purely physical and cosmetic reasons. But fasting has a deeply spiritual application.

Legitimate fasting always has a spiritual purpose. It is never presented in the Bible as having any value in and of itself. The only fast commanded in Scripture is the one connected with the Day of Atonement. They were to *"humble their souls" (Lev. 16:29)*. This is a Hebrew expression that includes forsaking food as an act of self-denial. Fasting is an entirely non-compulsory, voluntary act. It is not a spiritual duty to be regularly observed.

"Moreover when ye fast, be not, as the hypocrites, of a sad countenance: for they disfigure their faces, that they may appear unto men to fast. Verily I say unto you, they have their reward. But thou, when thou fastest, anoint thine head, and wash thy face; That thou appear not unto men to fast, but unto thy Father which is in secret: and thy Father, which seeth in secret, shall reward thee openly." (Matthew 6:16-18)

1. False Fasting (Matthew 6:16)

In Jesus' day, fasting had become a ritual to gain merit with God and attention before others. Many of the Pharisees fasted twice a week (Luke 18:12), usually on Monday and Thursday. It is claimed that those days were chosen because they were the days they thought Moses made the two separate trips to receive the tablets of law from God on Mt. Sinai. But those two days also happened to be big Jewish market days, when cities and towns were crowded with farmers, merchants, and shoppers. They were the two days with the largest audience.

People wanted to make sure others knew they were fasting. So, they would not wash their face or keep their hair. Some would sprinkle ashes on their head so people would know they were in mourning. These people would take great pains to make sure others knew they were fasting. But God took no notice. Since they fasted so people would notice, people were their only audience.

Jesus encourages fasting that seeks God's recognition, not that of others. Jesus is really teaching about our motivation. What motivates someone to fast or do any type of religious prohibition? I know people who will not go to movies, or work on Sunday, or wear certain clothing, or some other questionable activity. Jesus wants to make sure we have the proper motivation for denying ourselves. If our motivation is so others will think we are a better Christian, that's all we receive. Some people judge the validity of a person's Christianity on what is given up for Jesus. It is good to go without. Our motivation should always be to please God first. And if it pleases God, we do not need to try to amplify or broadcast our "sacrifice" for God.

2. Proper Fasting (Matthew 6:17-18)

Fasting is mentioned 30 times in the New Testament, almost always favorably. Fasting seems to be normal and acceptable in the Christian life. Jesus assumes His followers will fast on certain occasions, but He doesn't give a command or specify a particular time, place, or method.

Jesus' disciples did not fast while He was with them. Fasting is associated primarily with mourning or other times of overwhelming spiritual need or anxiety. Since Jesus was present, there was no need to fast. But for us, there are times when we are so burdened we need to refrain from eating and concentrate on God.

Fasting is never shown in Scripture to be the means to heightened spiritual experience, visions, or special insight or awareness — as many mystics, including some Christian mystics, claim. Fasting is appropriate in this age because Christ is physically absent from the earth. But it is appropriate only as a response to special times of testing, trial, and struggle. Fasting is the humbling of our body and soul before God.

When is fasting appropriate?

1. **Times of sorrow.** Fasting is many times an automatic reaction to a loss of a loved one in death or any time of great sadness. David refused to eat when his baby was near death (2 Samuel 12:16). Like David, we are too sad to eat. But sometimes we need to make ourselves eat to keep our strength.

2. **Overwhelming danger.** King Jehoshaphat proclaimed a fast when approached with an enemy (2 Chronicles 20:3) and Esther called for a fast before she was going to talk with the King about sparing the life of the Jews (Esther 4:16). When faced with a dangerous situation, fasting and prayer may help you gain strength and courage.

3. **Penitence**. When faced with judgment for sin, the people of Nineveh proclaimed a fast and everyone fasted and prayed for deliverance. (Jonah 3:5,7). If you are aware of a sin, one way to be delivered from the judgment against that sin is to fast and pray. God encouraged the sinful nation of Israel to *"turn ye even to me with all your heart, and with fasting, and with weeping, and with moaning..." (Joel 2:12).* The result? *"... for he is gracious and merciful, slow to anger, and of great kindness, and repenteth him of the evil." (Joel 2:13).*

4. **Beginning of an important task or ministry.** Before the initial cross-cultural missionary endeavor of the early church, the leaders spent time in fasting and prayer (Acts 13:2,3). Only the Lord knows how much the leadership of a church today could be strengthened if congregations were that determined to find and follow the Lord's will.

5. **Helping share in others in need.** One of the simple benefits of fasting is the ability to share what we might have eaten (or its cost) with the undernourished. If we had an occasional (or scheduled) fasting for lunch and missed a meal, it would free up money and time to do good for others.

6. **Practicing self-discipline.** Hunger is one of our basic human appetites and greed is one of our basic human sins. Self-control is the ability to control our bodies. Fasting is the activity of telling our self "No" to a natural bodily appetite. Fasting can give you the as-

surance that your body does not control you. You can control your body by surrendering it to God.

How should we fast?

Jesus explains that an appropriate fast is just the opposite of what the popular Pharisees were doing.

A person who fasts should do everything to make himself normal and do nothing to attract attention to his deprivation and spiritual struggle. The one who sincerely wants to please God will avoid trying to impress others.

Fasting is not to be a display for anyone, including God. We may get this silly notion that if I deprive myself before God, He will surely notice what I'm doing and help me. But you cannot impress God with your good works. We can bluff a human audience and they can be taken in by our performances. But God is not mocked. We can't deceive Him. God hates hypocrisy but loves reality.

A proper fast, however, is not to go in the other extreme. We are not to appear overly happy at our fasting. We are not to abandon one form of hypocrisy to embrace another form of hypocrisy. He says we should act normal.

The purpose of fasting is not to advertise our self but to discipline our self. It is not to gain a reputation for us but to express our humility before God and our concern for others in need.

Fasting is linked with prayer. You can pray without fasting, but you cannot fast Biblically without praying

Fasting is also linked to a pure heart. It is associated with obedient, godly living. In Zechariah 7:5-10, God made remarks about the fasting of the Jews during their 70 years in Babylon. They were going through the motions, but did not have the right motivation. He asked the Jews, *"...When ye fasted and mourned... did ye at all fast unto me, even to me?"* God then mentioned what should have been the result of their fasting. "Execute true judgment, and show mercy and compassions every man to his brother: and oppress not the widow, nor the fatherless, the stranger, nor the poor: and let none of you imagine evil against his brother in his heart." This is what was missing in the fasting of the Pharisees. Fasting did not change their behavior. Don't let good behavior be missing as you fast.

I hope these thoughts help you in your Christian journey. Fasting provides an opportunity to practice self-discipline to draw closer to Jesus Christ and administer grace to others.

CHAPTER TWENTY:

MAKE YOUR BEST FINANCIAL INVESTMENT

M ONEY IS IMPORTANT to people. I remember a funny story about riches...

On a secluded island a lone pirate was captured who couldn't speak English. The captain of the ship told his interpreter to say, "Tell him if he doesn't tell us where they have hidden all of their gold, we will make him walk the plank." Through the interpreter, the pirate responded, "I'd rather die than tell you where the gold is hidden" The captain tied the pirate's hand together and led him to the side of the ship." The pirate again responded, "I'd rather die than tell you where the gold is." With that, the captain pushed him to the end of the plank. Sharks were just 5 feet below. The captain said to the interpreter, "Tell him if he doesn't tell us where the gold is, we will push him off the plank." The pirate could stand it no longer and said, "The gold is hidden in a little cave on the island just behind the large waterfall. The waterfall is one mile over the hill to the right." The interpreter related the following to the captain, "He said that he would rather die than tell you where the gold is." Many people will sacrifice anything for a little more money.

Not only is money important to people, but it may surprise you that money is important to God. Jesus talked a great deal about money. Sixteen of His thirty-eight parables were concerned with how to handle money and possessions. In the Gospels, an amazing one out of 10 verses (288 in all) deals directly with the subject of money. The Bible offers 500 verses on prayer, less than 500 verses on faith, but more than 2,000 verses on money and possessions.

If money and our possessions are so important, we surely want to keep them secure. We want to make sure what we have will last. If you have any investments, you make sure what you have is kept safe. You lock your home and your cars to keep people from taking what you have. Even an unlocked bike isn't safe in some neighborhoods. But even if you feel you have protected your money and stuff as best you can, anything can happen. And in the end, you have to leave it all; you die.

When John D. Rockefeller, Sr. died, someone asked the accountant one day, "How much did John D. leave? We know he was an immensely wealthy man." Without a moment's hesitation, the accountant answered, "Everything!"

When you die, you will leave behind everything. It's been said "You can't take it with you." But can you? I like what Rick Warren has said many time, "You can't take it with you but you can send it on ahead." The Bible says we can have treasure in heaven.

"Lay not up for yourselves treasures upon earth, where moth and rust doth corrupt, and where thieves break through and steal: But lay up for yourselves treasures in heaven, where neither moth nor rust doth corrupt, and where thieves do not break through nor steal: For where your treasure is, there will your heart be also." (Matthew 6:19-21)

Whenever you meet with an investment banker, he or she will ask you several questions. How much money would you like to invest? How much risk are you willing to take with your investment? What is the purpose for investment — short or long term?

As we consider Jesus' comments on money and possessions, He talks about investing these for eternity. I think we can ask ourselves three questions that will help us know if we are making a good investment for eternity: (1) Which bank will you use? (2) What attitude will you have as you invest? (3) Who is your master? Your answer to these questions will determine if your treasure is in Heaven.

Two Banks: Heaven or Earth

The Bank of Earth. Such things as decay, depreciation, and theft constantly threaten riches and possessions on earth. Jesus reminds us that nothing we own is completely safe. People can steal what we have. Time can damage what we have. Things get old and worn out. The value of things doesn't last. It has been said, "I can't think of anything that's as much fun to own as it is to look forward to owning." The more a person has, the more they worry about moths, and worms, and rust. And even if we keep our possessions perfectly secure during our entire lives, we are certainly separated from them at death (Job 1:21). This is a poor investment.

The Bank of Heaven. Possessions that are used for God's purposes can be a means of accumulating heavenly possessions. There are only two places to store treasure. When done for the Lord, we can build up heavenly treasures that are completely free from destruction or theft. Jesus suggests heaven because it lasts longer, the vaults are more secure, and the banker more reliable. This is God's formula for earning dividends that are both guaranteed and permanent. This is a great investment.

Martin Luther said, "God divided the hands into fingers so that money could slip through." Laying up treasure in heaven is to do anything on earth whose effects last for eternity.

So how does this work? When we get to Heaven do we get a bankbook or credit card with a balance of cash we can spend in Heaven's Coffee Shop? I do not think that money works this way. While I am not sure what Heaven is like, I know that values will change. There will be blessings and rewards received for how we spent what God gave us. If we spent our time, talent, experiences, relationships, treasure, and gifts for God we will receive the investment with interest.

When I recently traveled to South Korea, I took quite a bit of money. But when I got to the country, I had to trade my dollars for won, the Korean currency, in order to purchase anything. In the same way, your dollars need to be exchanged for you to have rewards in Heaven. You exchange these by using them for Jesus.

Please be aware that this is not a ban on possessions. Some people have mistakenly suggested that we are not to put our money in savings for another day. They think it is a lack of faith and trust. Saving is not forbidden in the Bible. The ant is presented as a good example because he stores food for a later date (Proverbs 6:6). We are not to despise what God has given, but enjoy God's blessings. Instead of feeling guilty, we should be grateful and generous to others. (1 Timothy 4:3-4; 6:17). When you have more, you can give more. What Jesus is warning about is the selfish accumulation of stuff just to have stuff. Do not accumulate possessions simply for your own sake. If you have more than you need, invest it in eternity.

Two Attitudes: Now or Later

I can remember the Fram oil commercial on television. A mechanic had a car engine torn apart. The cost was over $2,000. A Fram oil filter could have prevented it for only

$5. His comment: "You can pay me now. Or you can pay me later."

I think we need to consider this with our money and possessions. Do we want it now or do we want it forever? It is such a temptation to grab what we can now when we can get it. Why wait till later? I think Jesus illustrates this concept with a "good" and "bad" eye.

"The light of the body is the eye: if therefore thine eye be single, thy whole body shall be full of light. But if thine eye be evil, thy whole body shall be full of darkness. If therefore the light that is in thee be darkness, how great is that darkness!" (Matthew 6:22-23).

Your eye is important to your whole body. I have needed glasses since I was in 8th grade. Without my glasses, I can't drive, recognize people from a distance, or even read a road sign. A good eye will help you see everything clearly and make good decisions.

However, a bad ("dark") eye leads to poor choices because we can't see clearly. I remember once I had an infection in both eyes and needed to take medicine so they could get better. It affected everything. I cannot imagine what it would be like to be blind.

When you see life, as it really is, a temporary assignment, you will make good choices. You will choose to spend what you have in things that will last. I like how Jesus talks about a "single" eye. When you have focus on the important things, you get important things done. But when you get distracted, you get very little accomplished. All the stuff of life can get you distracted from what is of eternal value. Don't let your stuff determine your decisions. Let eternity determine your decisions.

When a person invests on earth, he makes poor choices. He's only looking for immediate results. But when a person invests in heaven, he makes wiser choices with his possessions. He's looking for the long-term results of his decisions.

Two Masters: Jesus or Money

Just as we cannot have our treasures on earth and heaven, or have our riches both now and later, we cannot follow two masters.

"No man can serve two masters: for either he will hate the one, and love the other; or else he will hold to the one, and despise the other. Ye cannot serve God and mammon (money)."(Matthew 6:24)

People can work for two employers, but no slave can be the property of two owners. To try to share Jesus with other loyalties is idolatry. It is like loving two women. You can, but once you love one, you have sacrificed the love of the other. You are either a slave to Christ or sin (Rom. 6:16-22).

Notice Jesus didn't say it's bad to serve two masters. He said you can't serve two masters. It's impossible. Here is where the old adage applies, "If Jesus isn't Lord of all, He isn't Lord at all."

In addition, notice our choices. Our choice isn't God or the Devil. Our choice is God or our money (and the things that money buys). Jesus says the #1 competition God has for your heart is your money. But God isn't really interested in getting your money. God doesn't need your money. He is interested in your heart. So, that is why He talks so much about money. He wants your heart.

This is really what it boils down to — Who is your boss? Who determines how you live your life? Who determines your decisions? Is it Jesus or something else? If Jesus is not your boss, you will have everything else in your life trying to tell you what to do. And you will be stressed out. But if Jesus is the boss of your life, it may be difficult at times, but life becomes clear and simple. And simple is a great way to live.

Sigmund Freud's favorite story was about the sailor shipwrecked on an island. He was seized by the natives, hoisted to their shoulders, carried to the village, and set on a throne. He learned that it was their custom once each year to make some man a king for a year. He liked it until he began to wonder what happened to all the former kings. Soon he discovered that every year when his kingship was ended, the king was banished to an island, where he starved to death. The sailor did not like that, but he was smart and he was king for a year. So, he put his carpenters to work making boats, his farmers to work transplanting fruit trees to the island, farmers growing crops, masons building houses. So, when his kingship was over, he was banished, not to a barren island, but to an island of abundance. It is a good parable of life: We're all kings here, kings for a little while, able to choose what we shall do with the stuff of life. "Lay not up for yourselves treasures on earth... but lay up for yourselves treasures in heaven..."

CHAPTER TWENTY-ONE:

DON'T WORRY

WORRY. WE ALL do it. It's been said, "Worry does not take away tomorrow's troubles. It takes away today's peace." Another said, "Worry is like a rocking chair. It will give you something to do. But it won't get you anywhere." One more: "Worry won't stop the bad stuff from happening. It just stops you from enjoying the good stuff."

In Jesus' Sermon on the Mount, he speaks about worry. Jesus made an honest evaluation of the things that concern every person. Jesus noted that we worry about life, our needs, and our future. I think we all know it, but we shouldn't worry. But we do anyway. Jesus helps us stop worrying.

"Therefore I say unto you, Take no thought for your life, what ye shall eat, or what ye shall drink; nor yet for your body, what ye shall put on. Is not the life more than meat, and the body than raiment? Behold the fowls of the air: for

they sow not, neither do they reap, nor gather into barns; yet your heavenly Father feedeth them. Are ye not much better than they? Which of you by taking thought can add one cubit unto his stature? And why take ye thought for raiment? Consider the lilies of the field, how they grow; they toil not, neither do they spin: And yet I say unto you, That even Solomon in all his glory was not arrayed like one of these. Wherefore, if God so clothe the grass of the field, which today is, and tomorrow is cast into the oven, shall he not much more clothe you, O ye of little faith? Therefore take no thought, saying, What shall we eat? or, What shall we drink? or, Wherewithal shall we be clothed? (For after all these things do the Gentiles seek:) for your heavenly Father knoweth that ye have need of all these things." (Matthew 6:25-32)

Three reasons we should not worry...

1- Worry is not productive — "Can worry add anything to your life?"

The English word "worry" comes from the German word "worgen" and means "to strangle." Worry strangles us. The Greek word is a combination of two words meaning "to divide" and "the mind." Worry causes a divided mind. Worry is like a dense fog. The other Sunday morning we had fog until near noon. It caused people to be late to church because they had to drive slowly. Worry does that. It slows down progress and causes accidents.

Jesus uses a similar word when He shares the "Parable of the Sower" in Mark 4. If you remember, the sower threw some seeds in various locations. In one location, the seed was "strangled" by some weeds (Mark 4:18-19). This is the same word. Worry strangles us.

Another time Jesus uses the word is when He is with Mary and Martha. Mary was sitting, listening to Jesus while her sister Martha was working. Martha complained to Jesus. But Jesus said that Martha was *"careful and troubled about many things"* (Luke 10:41). Same word. Worry causes us to be troubled about too many things.

Do you find yourself unable to sleep because you are thinking about all the things that need to be done? In Jesus' words, you are *"careful and troubled about many things."* That's what worry does and it isn't productive. Most of the things we worry about never happen.

2- Worry is not necessary — 'Won't God do more for you than the flowers and grass?'

God is Master of everything. He knows everything and He owns everything (Ps. 24:1). He also controls everything (1 Chron. 29:12). He provides for everything we need (Phil. 4:19). Since He is responsible for everything, don't you think He will take care of it? I don't think God is worried about our finances, or our health, or our children, or our job, or our broken-down car, or our country? He knows exactly what is going on. We can trust God to take care of it. Our worry won't change anything, and therefore, is not necessary.

God takes care of His own. Jesus compares humanity with all of nature. God has provided a wonderful illustration all around us of His care.

The birds work and labor for their food. But they do not hoard or stockpile. God put within nature the ability for them to be fed throughout the year. And He even provides kind-hearted people, like my mother-in-law, who give them food in the winter. God takes care of the birds.

The flowers and vegetation are beautiful. In Michigan, people take color tours throughout the state just to see the changing leaves in the Fall. I remember driving through the Smoky Mountains in the Spring to see the blooming rhododendrons along the mountainsides. It was just beautiful. God has clothed all of nature in unmatched beauty. God takes care of His world.

If God feeds the birds and clothes the plants, He has promised He will take care of us. These are simply His creation, but we are His children. He surely will take care of us. No need to worry.

However, people are hungry. And many go without clothes or shelter. Why? Has God broken His promise? It is not inadequate provision, but unequal distribution. Some hoard, while others do without.

3- Worry is not worthy — 'Isn't life more than food and aren't you worth more than birds?'

You are more than just a body to maintain. You have significance. You are more than the fulfillments of your appetites. Your needs are more than physical. You have a deeper need.

Everybody has ambitions. We are not like algae drifting out at sea. We need something to live for, to give meaning to our existence. It is what makes us get up in the morning. It's what makes us "tick."

We all have a motivation. Some choose "material security." So, they go out and make all the money they can, buy all they stuff they can, save all the stuff they can, and then just sit on the can.

Others choose God's kingdom. They live for a higher purpose and have a deeper meaning to their life. Life is more than food, clothing and shelter. Life is more than just getting my needs met. Life is living in such a way that God is pleased with it. That is where it's at.

So, worry is not worthy because we were created for more. And worry is not worthy because God is better than that. At its core, worry strikes a blow at both God's love and God's integrity. We can only worry when we doubt God's unconditional love for us and His ability to do what He says. Worry affects our trust in God.

How to stop worry...

"But seek ye first the kingdom of God, and His righteous-
ness; and all these things will be added unto you. Take
therefore no thought for the morrow: for the morrow shall
take thought for the things of itself. Sufficient unto the day
is the evil thereof." (Matthew 6:33-34)

Jesus ends His discussion on worry with two applications.
Two simple things you can do to eliminate worry. They are
simple but not easy.

1. **Put first things first.** Jesus is concerned with the
    priorities of our life. Most of us have a lot going on.
    But Jesus commands that our first priority be His
    kingdom and His righteousness.

    Seeking God's Kingdom means Jesus rules your life.
    This begins by trusting Jesus as Lord and Savior. It
    is also a call to be involved in bringing people into
    His kingdom.

    Seeking God's Righteousness is a broader concept.
    Because God is righteous, He desires righteousness
    in every human community, not just Christian. We
    are to make His righteousness attractive so others
    will desire it. Live it and encourage it.

    Seeking this first is not easy. Everything in my life
    screams for first place. And many of these things are
    very good things, like my family, my ministry, my

health, and my wife. But Jesus promised that if He is first, everything else will fall into place.

The word "priority" is interesting. We talk about having many priorities. But when the word was first introduced in the 1600s, it was only singular. And this makes sense. "Priority" comes from the word "prior," which means "coming before in time, order or importance." You can have many things that are important, but you can only have one "First." That is your priority. What is your priority?

2. **Live one day at a time.** This has to do with simplicity. Life is not meant to be complicated. If you have more to do than you have time to do it, you are doing more than God intended. Worry only adds to your stress.

    Jesus warns us about "double worry." Tomorrow has enough trouble. Don't contaminate today by corrupting it with tomorrow's troubles. If we worry, we double what we worry about. If our fear doesn't materialize, we worried for nothing. If it does, we worried twice instead of once. In both cases, it is foolish. And I've often found that things are usually not as bad as I thought they'd be.

    Jesus encourages us to do it today. Do what needs to be done and do it well. I mentioned earlier about Mary and Martha. In Luke 10:38-42, Martha was worried and bothered. Jesus told her that one thing was needed. At the time, I think the one thing that was needed was to sit at the feet of Jesus and listen to Him teach. Cooking and cleaning could wait. Often in life, we can simplify things by asking, "What one thing can I do now that will make the most impact?" Certain things need to be done. Get them done and concentrate on God and His Kingdom. And never underestimate the importance of one task.

Worry is the sin of not trusting the promise and providence of God. Worry shows that we are mastered by our circumstances and by our own perspectives and understanding rather than by God. Some worry is good (pressure or concern might be a better word). We meet deadlines, prepare for an assignment, get medical check-ups, all because we are concerned about something. Some people worry about us and push us to do positive things that better our life. Jesus was warning against destructive worry, especially about material possessions. Jesus is not discouraging forethought and planning, but rather about nervous anxiety and unneeded stress.

Worry cannot change the future. We simply must leave that in God's hands. If you are not sure that you have accepted Christ as Savior, you can do that today and leave all your tomorrows in His hands. If you have accepted Christ as Savior, and yet are worrying about your tomorrows, that's not your job. Leave your troubles in the hands of the Savior. He will take care of them and you.

CHAPTER TWENTY TWO:

DON'T CRITICIZE

WE'VE ALL HEARD someone say, "Don't judge me." We have probably used this phrase ourselves many times. It is not only based on Jesus' famous Sermon on the Mount (Matthew 7:1-6), it is also a natural reaction when we receive criticism from others. When we hear a critical remark about some offensive action we have taken, it rubs us the wrong way. No one likes to have his or her faults pointed out. So, rather than accept the criticism and try to understand any truth behind it, we often deflect any wrongdoing onto the critical person. It's a lot easier to blame someone else for judging than work to see our own faults.

No matter what people say, we can't change their critical attitudes toward us. It is human nature to point out the flaws in others. But we can curb the criticism we hold toward other people.

So, what's wrong with criticism? While there is a place for constructive criticism, I discovered four reasons criticism (judging others) should be discouraged.

1. We never know all the facts. It is so easy to make a quick assessment of a situation without knowing everything. Maybe if we knew all the other person had been through in his or her life, we might be a little more understanding.

2. We are unable to read another's motive. We don't know why someone does something. We try to understand, but we don't know the motives of others.

3. We are prejudiced people, never completely objective. Our own history has a tendency to color our experience. If you have had a bad experience with men, or women, or a certain ethnicity, or vocation, you will tend to view others of that group in the same light. So, we need to be careful that our own preconceived ideas are not clouding our criticism. It might not be them. We might be the ones who need some alteration.

4. We put ourselves in a position we are not qualified to fill, namely, we play God. We are not the judge. Even if we are a judge by employment, we are not the ultimate judge. We can only make decisions based on facts. So, when we judge another person, we are setting ourselves up as an authority that we may not own. Sometimes we are demanded to make a decision on a preconceived rule (like a sports referee or law enforcement person or parent). But we need to

remind ourselves that the ultimate judge will judge us. So, we'd better lean toward leniency if we want that from Him.

Christians are often guilty of judging others. Though we are called by God to proclaim the truth and help others trapped in sin, it is the duty of every Christian to check attitudes before voicing any criticism. It was such a prevalent issue in Jesus' day that He talked about judging others in the Sermon on the Mount.

"Judge not, that ye be not judged. For with what judgment ye judge, ye shall be judged: and with what measure ye mete, it shall be measured to you again. And why beholdest thou the mote that is in thy brother's eye, but considerest not the beam that is in thine own eye? Or how wilt thou say to thy brother, Let me pull out the mote out of thine eye; and, behold, a beam is in thine own eye? Thou hypocrite, first cast out the beam out of thine own eye; and then shalt thou see clearly to cast out the mote out of thy brother's eye. Give not that which is holy unto the dogs, neither cast ye your pearls before swine, lest they trample them under their feet, and turn again and rend you." (Matthew 7:1-6)

Jesus presents two reasons why we shouldn't criticize (judge) others.

1. The attitude we demonstrate will be the one that returns to us (Luke 6:36-38). Criticism is like a boomerang. It finds its way back to us. Those who judge will be judged by the same standards they used to judge others. I should treat others the way I want to

be treated. Before you confront someone about their sin, try to put yourself in their shoes. "If it were me, how would I want someone to approach me?"

2. Judging is hypocritical. Judging tends to magnify our virtues and others' vices. It is easy to criticize someone in an area that we are doing well at. But we would not want someone to come to the same conclusion with an issue we struggle against. Yet, even if we find our own faults in others, we judge them anyway. It may be that we know we are wrong and deserve to be scolded, so we feel better scolding others. James reminds us that we are especially guilty when we do not practice what we ourselves teach and preach (James 3:1). We often see our criticism as an act of righteousness, not what it really is, sin. Jesus teaches that the sin of pride in the critic is much greater than the sin in the person he is criticizing. It is interesting to note that this is the only time disciples are called hypocrites in the Sermon on the Mount.

Jesus teaches a healthy balance between judging and discernment.

Though Jesus tells us not to judge, some have misinterpreted this command. Some have used this Bible passage to defend unbiblical behavior. It's as if we are not to determine someone is wrong. If this is true, Jesus didn't listen to His own sermon because He criticized others (example – Matthew 23).

Taken to an extreme, not judging would mean we don't help others with personal struggles or moral failures. Before a doctor can treat someone's illness, there must be an honest assessment and diagnosis of the problem. Similarly, before a person can be free from the grips of a sinful habit or action, there must be an acceptance that it is sin. Often a confrontation must occur. To use this passage to deflect any help to overcome sin is foolish. It is true we are not to judge others in condemnation. Only God can determine the eternal destiny of a person. But we are not to ignore their faults. We still have a responsibility to our "brother" (Matt. 18:15).

This same paragraph in the Sermon on the Mount that commands us "Judge not", also tells us to "remove the speck out of our brother's eye." This means that if we notice even something small in the life of someone that needs to be removed, we are commanded to help get rid of it. Yet, before we approach them, we need to self-check to make sure our bigger problem isn't clouding our perception. If you have a log in your eye, you really aren't in a place to see a speck clearly. Our Christian duty is to take out the log in our own eye so we can see better to take out the speck out of another's eye.

I hope this makes sense because this is the balance. We are commanded to help others live the life God blesses. But when we don't deal with our own problems, it is easy to work on the problems of others. As we work on our own issues, it is amazing how clearly and compassionately we can see the problems of others. And sometimes the experience of removing our problems will give insight to others to remove their own problems.

Jesus is not condemning criticism. But He is attacking criticism without self-criticism. If we confess our sin, we will see everything clearly. Never put your finger on someone else's faults unless it's part of a helping hand.

Some are habitually critical of others. I've known people that cannot give a compliment, but are able, willing, and enthusiastic to criticize anything they don't agree with in another. If this is you, please curb this habit.

Pigs and Pearls

Jesus finishes this section with an admonition not to cast pearls to swine. For most of us, this sounds ridiculous. And it is. No one would take something valuable and give it to someone who doesn't appreciate its value. Neither should we. He also mentions not giving something holy to dogs. But why does Jesus teach this immediately following His comments on judging?

Jesus teaches this lesson on pigs, pearls, dogs and holiness to show the difference between judging and discernment. We just read five verses about not judging, but Jesus reminds us we do need to have some discernment to know what is a pig and a dog. In Jesus' day, pigs and dogs were often used as a reference to those who were not in relationship with God (2 Peter 2:22). It was also used for those who have no discernment: *"As dog returneth to his vomit, so a fool returneth to his folly" (Proverbs 26:11).* Dogs will eat anything. Pigs will eat slop. So, the parable teaches that we are to have discernment and not give something good and holy to those who do not appreciate it.

This does not mean we are not to tell others without the Gospel the good news of Jesus Christ. Jesus talked with sinners (Matthew 9:10). In another teaching, Jesus tells His disciples to leave the home or city of people who don't accept them (Matthew 10:14). We are to share the gospel and the truth of God's Word, but if it is not welcome, we are to move on. As pigs don't appreciate pearls, some people don't appreciate the truth of God's Word. Our job is not to force the truth down people's throat. Our job is to share the truth with those who are ready to hear it.

How can I stop the habit of criticism?

Criticism can be a hard habit to break. I know people who feel compelled to be a food critic in every restaurant they attend. I think they've watched too much Food Network. Life would be much simpler if we concentrated on our own faults, and only pointed out the faults of others if they were in serious danger.

So, if you are serious about curbing your critical attitude, I have found a few insights. I hope this helps. I know they will help your relationships with others.

1. Examine yourself before being tempted to inspect others.

2. Confess your faults before confronting another.

3. Try to understand the other person's struggle. We must be tender and gentle.

4. Remember, the goal is restoration, not probation. We are dealing with family members.

CHAPTER TWENTY-THREE:

LOVE PEOPLE

WHEN I WAS in Bible College, I worked at a turkey processing plant. We had a saying, "It's hard to soar with eagles when you work with turkeys." Though that is comical, it is often true.

I think most of us realize that relationships are what make or break anything. If you can't get along with others, life can be miserable. However, if you are surrounded with people you love and who love you, you can handle about anything.

In our previous lesson from Matthew 7:1-6, we discovered the negative side of relationships. It shows the negative response when we are shown to be wrong. We tend to be critical and point an accusing finger at other people. When relationships break down, a vicious cycle of hurt occurs.

However, Matthew 7:7-12 gives the positive side of relationships. It gives the reason the previous response is wrong. When we put ourselves first, we end up hurting relationships. But when we think of others, we will repair and mend relationships.

"Ask, and it shall be given you; seek, and ye shall find; knock, and it shall be opened unto you: For every one that asketh receiveth; and he that seeketh findeth; and to him that knocketh it shall be opened. Or what man is there of you, whom if his son ask bread, will he give him a stone? Or if he ask a fish, will he give him a serpent? If ye then, being evil, know how to give good gifts unto your children, how much more shall your Father which is in heaven give good things to them that ask him? Therefore all things whatsoever ye would that men should do to you, do ye even so to them: for this is the law and the prophets." (Matthew 7:7-12)

This section concludes with one of the most famous Bible passages in the world, the Golden Rule: "Therefore all things whatsoever ye would that men should do to you, do ye even so to them: for this is the law and the prophets."

The Golden Rule (Matthew 7:12) has been called the Mount Everest of Ethics. Application of the Golden Rule settles a hundred issues. It prevents the necessity of laying down endless little rules for our conduct in specific cases. If we live life according to the Golden Rule, we will find our relationships will be blessed.

But before Jesus gives the Golden Rule He has a comment on prayer. He relates prayer to relationships. Prior to prayer, Jesus talked about relationships, and following prayer Jesus talked about relationships. So right in the middle of Jesus' commentary on relationships, He uses prayer as an illustration.

In combining prayer and relationships, it's as if Jesus is saying, "If your heavenly Father is kind to you even though you have faults, shouldn't you be kind and generous to others though they have faults?" We should treat others like we want God to treat us. We should treat others like we want to be treated.

There are three reasons you should love other people like yourself.

1. **God's Promises** — We can love others without fear of depleting the divine resources. God promises to answer.

    Jesus emphasizes the need for perseverance in prayer. In the Greek, the tense of the verb indicates a continuous action. For example, in prayer we should "keep on asking, keep on seeking, keep on knocking."

    Notice the intensity of the three verbs: ask, seek, knock. If someone is near, we may ask him or her. If we ask, and they are not near, we may go seeking for them to ask. If we still can't find them, we may need to knock on a door to see if they are inside. Often our prayers seem like God is not listening. But sometimes God intentionally hides His answer until we are ready.

I remember when my daughter wanted to get her ears pierced. My wife and I talked it over, and we felt she wasn't old enough or responsible enough to take care of them. But the more she asked and asked and asked, we realized this was something she would carry through with. It was her persistence that made us realize that she was ready.

God already knows if we are ready to receive a request or not. Sometimes He withholds the answer so we can know we aren't ready. I am so glad God has not given me everything I've prayed for. I thought I was ready. But looking back, I know I was not.

It would appear from this verse that you will always eventually get that for which you ask, seek and knock. But this one verse is not a blank check to ask for whatever you want. This is not meant to be a thorough teaching on prayer. This verse teaches that God is a Father who wants to give His children good gifts. So, we can feel confident to ask, seek, or knock.

A key danger of false teachers is to build a doctrine on one verse of Scripture. Many doctrinal errors have been made by taking one verse out of context or by not comparing one Scripture with the rest of the Bible. We must look at many other scriptures to understand prayer.

Please note these other qualifications of answered prayer:

- **Born-again**. Since Jesus refers to God as Father, only those who are born spiritually can come to God as a Father. Those who are not His children cannot come to Him as Father.

- **Obedience**. *"And whatsoever we ask, we receive of him, because we keep his commandments, and do those things that are pleasing in his sight." (1 John 3:22).*

- **Right motive.** *"Ye ask, and receive not, because ye ask amiss, that ye may consume it upon your lusts." (James 4:3).*

- **Submissive to His will.** *"And this is the confidence that we have in him, that, if we ask any thing according to his will, he heareth us:" (1 John 5:14).*

- **God's Pattern.** We are to love others because God does. (also Ephesians 5:1-2)

In talking about God as Father, Jesus uses the Greek word "Abba." This was the everyday, family word. It is like our word "Daddy." Jesus reminds us that God is our Father. It is not natural for a father to ignore the needs of his son. Even though we may be sinful and far from perfect, we still meet needs of those we love if we can. God does the same. He is a perfect Father and has the power to meet every need. Evidently, if my needs aren't met, it wasn't a need in the first place.

Some may question, "If our Father is going to give it to us anyway, why ask?" God's giving depends on our asking not because he is ignorant or reluctant. The question is not whether He is ready to give, but whether we are ready to receive. God never spoils His children. He does not give us gifts whether we want them or not, or whether we are ready or not.

God often gives to those who don't ask and fails to give to many who do. Being good, He gives good gifts. Being wise, He knows what gifts are good. Some gifts that appear to be good are really not. And often it takes time to see the goodness in a gift.

But be reminded that sometimes we fail to receive because we do not ask. "... Ye have not because ye ask not." (James 4:2). So, go ahead and ask your Father and trust Him to give you what you need when you need it.

2. **God's Purposes** – The Golden Rule is the best-known of Jesus' teachings and the highest level of His ethical teaching.

   This is not the first time in history that similar statements were made. Many philosophers spoke about treating others the way we wanted to be treated. But prior to Jesus, they were always dealing with negative actions.

   Confucius said, "What you do not want done to yourself, do not do to others." Jesus gave a superior teaching by shifting from the negative to the positive. To adhere to Confucius' teaching, we can simply leave others alone. We simply don't do bad things to other people. Honestly, if people would follow this, the world would be a better place. We would have no murder, lying, hatred, anger, rape, stealing, and many other vices. The police and all law enforcement would be out of business. This is a great rule of life. However, it is not enough. The mere absence of hatred does not constitute love.

Jesus had a superior rule. Treat others the way we want to be treated places our actions in the positive. We cannot merely sit by and do nothing. We must take action to help.

Yet, how we treat others is not to be determined simply by how we expect them to treat us or by how we think they should treat us. For example, I am an Ohio State Buckeye fan. For my birthday, I would be thrilled if someone gave me a Buckeye T-shirt. If I treat my Michigan Wolverine fan friend the way I want to be treated, I might give him a Buckeye shirt. But he won't be happy. I should do to him what I want done to me if I were him. I need to see my action from his perspective and ask "What would I want done to me?" This means we need to understand the other person. We may need to get to know them better. The book, Five Love Languages by Gary Chapman, has helped me greatly. Not everyone gives and receives love the same way. I need to love others the way they would want to receive it.

Only Jesus can take a negative aspect of our personality and make it positive. We are all basically selfish. We think of ourselves too much. It is natural. But we can use this tendency in an unselfish way. All we have to do is use our imagination. Put yourself in the other person's shoes and ask, "How would I like to be treated in this situation?" This is such a wise understanding of life.

Only Jesus can give power to live this kind of life. To think of others first is not natural. It is supernatural. I hope you will begin to see and receive the blessing of living for God and others.

I have developed three philosophies of life for how I treat other people. I repeat these to myself every morning before I leave my home for the day. I have yet to fully experience them. But hopefully I'm getting better. I want to treat every person I meet this way. Because people are under stress all around me and they really matter, I leave every person I speak to better than I found them because I genuinely care about what is happening in their lives.

- I will treat every person I meet the way I want to be treated.

- I will treat every person I meet the way I would treat Jesus if they were Him.

- I will treat every person I meet the way Jesus has treated me.

CHAPTER TWENTY-FOUR:

MAKE THE RIGHT CHOICE

L IFE IS MADE up of many decisions. Some are simple. But even simple decisions can be difficult, like what flavor of ice cream you want. Two children asked the lady at the ice cream counter why they only had chocolate and vanilla ice cream. She said, "If you knew how long it took people just to make up their mind from these two, you wouldn't want any more choices."

It is said that on top of a hill in a Midwestern state stands a courthouse so situated that raindrops falling on one side of the roof travel by way of the Great Lakes into the Atlantic Ocean. Raindrops landing on the opposite side of the roof find their way through the Ohio River and the Mississippi River to the Gulf of Mexico. Just a breath of wind one way or the other may determine whether a single raindrop will end up either in the Gulf of Mexico or in the Atlantic Ocean.

Even so, one single decision is enough to determine a person's life and even eternal destination. At the end of the greatest sermon ever given, Jesus asked His listeners to make a decision. This is life's ultimate choice. Jesus is drawing a line in the life of His listeners and says, "Will you cross this line and make the decision to follow Me?"

Jesus uses four illustrations to show what this eternal decision actually means.

First, what road will you travel on?

"Enter ye in at the strait gate: for wide is the gate, and broad is the way, that leadeth to destruction, and many there be which go in thereat: Because strait is the gate, and narrow is the way, which leadeth unto life, and few there be that find it." (Matthew 7:13-14)

Will you take the wide or narrow road of life? There are only two roads to choose — one seems easy, the other hard. They are entered by only two gates — one is wide, the other narrow. No matter how narrow or difficult, the best road is the road of Jesus.

Most people choose the wide road. It is the popular road. But the road Jesus encourages us to travel is only occupied by a few. Will you be one of the few?

But some may ask, "Don't all roads lead to Heaven?" The answer is "No." Each road ends at only two opposite destinations — destruction or life.

Second, what prophet will you listen to?

"Beware of false prophets, which come to you in sheep's clothing, but inwardly they are ravening wolves. Ye shall know them by their fruits. Do men gather grapes of thorns, or figs of thistles? Even so every good tree bringeth forth good fruit; but a corrupt tree bringeth forth evil fruit. A good tree cannot bring forth evil fruit, neither can a corrupt tree bring forth good fruit. Every tree that bringeth not forth good fruit is hewn down, and cast into the fire. Wherefore by their fruits ye shall know them." (Matthew 7:15-20)

Will you listen to the true prophet or the false prophet? Many think a false prophet is one who preaches a false gospel. Yes, that is true. But you can also tell a false teacher not by their words, but by their life. Do their works back up their words?

But some may ask "Aren't all ministers God's messengers?" The answer is "No." False prophets disguise themselves as God's messengers. Jesus warns us to beware. Not everyone who calls themselves a Christian minister or teacher is true to God. Be careful who you listen to.

Third, what destination are you moving toward?

"Not every one that saith unto me, Lord, Lord, shall enter into the kingdom of heaven; but he that doeth the will of my Father which is in heaven. Many will say to me in that day, Lord, Lord, have we not prophesied in thy name? and in thy name have cast out devils? and in thy name done many wonderful works? And then will I profess unto them, I never knew you: depart from me, ye that work iniquity." (Matthew 7:21-23)

There are only two final destinations, Heaven or Hell. Not everyone who does good deeds is going to Heaven. Many who are trying to get to Heaven by good works will be sadly disappointed when they stand before God. Good works are not required for Heaven.

But some may ask, "Aren't all good people going to Heaven?" The answer is "No." Only a relationship with Jesus will get a person to Heaven. Jesus said, "I am the way, the truth and the life; no man cometh unto the Father but by me." (John 14:6).

Fourth, what foundation are you building your life on? (Matthew 7:24-27)

"Therefore whosoever heareth these sayings of mine, and doeth them, I will liken him unto a wise man, which built his house upon a rock: And the rain descended, and the

floods came, and the winds blew, and beat upon that house; and it fell not: for it was founded upon a rock. And every one that heareth these sayings of mine, and doeth them not, shall be likened unto a foolish man, which built his house upon the sand: And the rain descended, and the floods came, and the winds blew, and beat upon that house; and it fell: and great was the fall of it." (Matthew 7:24-27)

There are only two foundations on which to build your life, sand or rock. Jesus uses a foundation as an illustration of what many people build their lives upon. The rock represents obedience to Jesus. The sand represents apathy toward what Jesus is saying.

We must not only hear what Jesus says, we must obey. To obey God is to believe in Jesus. God has commanded all people to repent and turn to Jesus as Lord and Savior. To obey is to believe.

But some may ask, "Does it really matter what you believe, as long as you are sincere?" The answer is "Yes it does matter." You can be sincerely wrong. Are you building your life on Jesus, the rock? Or are you building your life on the moving sand of others.

The Devil would like you to think that you are okay as long as you are doing some good things. He would have you believe that God would never send a good person to Hell. But he wants to deceive you until it is too late. Make the right choice today.

Following their first successful flight at Kitty Hawk, the Wright brothers telegrammed their family and told them all about it. They informed them that they would be home in time for the holidays. Their family reported all this to the local newspaper. The following week the article was entitled, "Local bicycle merchants will be home for the Holidays." The newspaper editor thought what was newsworthy was the boys were coming home. But what has been remembered is the short air flight. That is similar to the thinking of many good people today. They are concerned about their good works. But God is looking at the one area of obedience: Turning to Christ for salvation.

Turn today and follow and lead others to follow Jesus.

About the Author

Greg Burdine has been the senior pastor of Faith Baptist Church in Adrian, Michigan since 1994. He has been in pastoral ministry since 1982 and has served churches in Iowa, Ohio and Michigan. His passion is to help people understand and implement Biblical wisdom into their daily life. He has been married to his wife, Judy, since 1981 and has four grown children and seven grandchildren. Greg has an earned doctorate from Louisiana Baptist University. Beyond ministry, Greg loves to read, run and spend time with his family.